HAZEL'S

COOKIN' *with* COUNTRY STARS

★★★★

HOT DISH

Red Beans & Rice

Brooks & Dunn

Kix Brooks

2 pounds dried red kidney beans (soak overnight)
½ pound salt pork
4 fist-sized ham hocks (or more)
1 10" length pepperoni, sliced & quartered in ¾" chunks
hot Italian sausage links
1 10" length kielbasa
1 10" length smoked beef sausage
3-4 3" onions, diced (2 cups or more)
4 stalks celery, sliced diagonally
1½-2 cups green bell peppers, diced
1½-2 cups red bell peppers, diced
2-3 fresh tomatoes, sliced
2 28-ounce cans whole peeled tomatoes (use juice from one can only)
1 bunch green onions, chopped
1 29-ounce can tomato sauce
4-6 cloves garlic (if you use powder, cover the whole top with a layer)
3 tablespoons Tabasco® (or more)
½ teaspoon thyme
3 tablespoons Worcestershire sauce
1 teaspoon crushed red pepper
3 tablespoons cumin
½ tablespoon oregano (or more)
1 teaspoon pepper
1 tablespoon salt
1-1½ quarts of water

Rinse beans thoroughly, cover with water and soak overnight. Drain. Brown the Italian sausage links after removing the casings. In a large stock pot, combine beans, meats, and the remaining ingredients. Make sure beans and meat are covered with liquid. Bring to a boil and reduce heat to low. Cook 3–4 hours or until beans are tender. Adjust seasonings to taste. Remove ham bones and serve over rice.

Between interviews and video shoots, 2001

Pork Chops and Sauerkraut

Ronnie Dunn

4 butterfly porkchops
¼ cup butter
½ small onion, chopped
Cavender's™ seasoning mix
1 jar Vlasic® sauerkraut

Season porkchops generously with Cavender's™ and pepper. Sauté porkchops and onion together until brown. Add sauerkraut (partially drain liquid) and simmer for 1–2 hours. Serve with mashed potatoes and vegetables of your choice.

BR5-49

When I met these guys, I loved their vintage clothes, their songs, the big green guitar Chuck Mead played, and Gary Bennett's sexy vocals. I was crazy about the way Donnie Herron alternated from fiddle to steel to mandolin, singing harmony. Smiling Jay McDowell on bass was too cool, and Shaw Wilson with his Stoney Cooper looka-like moustache was absolutely charming.

Retro/hillbilly I call them: who else could open shows for the Black Crowes and Bob Dylan, be welcomed on the Grand Ole Opry and David Letterman, and do an award-winning commercial for Southwest Airlines?

They began at Robert's Western World, singing songs from Carl Smith, Faron Young, Hank Williams, Webb Pierce, etc. Crowds filled the tip jar and the club: a long-haired couple wearing tie-dyed shirts seated by an attorney in a three-piece suit, baby-faced college kids next to record execs next to a homeless wino who wandered in off the street. It was awesome.

Now on Sony, with singles like "Little Ramona" to their credit, they have worked their tails off on that hillbilly highway. Nothing could make me happier than seeing these five guys top the charts.

They began at Robert's Western World, singing songs from Carl Smith, Faron Young, Hank Williams, Webb Pierce, etc. Crowds filled the tip jar and the club.

Hillbilly Sushi

Donnie Herron of BR5-49

4 cups cooked sushi rice
⅛ cup sugar
2 teaspoons seasoned rice wine vinegar
½ teaspoon Jack Daniel's® whiskey (this puts the sue in sushi)

Mix these together.

1 pound salmon, sushi grade
2 carrots, cut into long, thin pieces
1 avocado, cut into long, thin pieces
2 celery sticks, cut into long, thin pieces
1 1-ounce can wasabi, dry
1 pack seaweed sheets (Nori®–has five full sheets)
½ cup sesame seeds
1 bamboo sushi roller

Put rice mixture on seaweed, then turn over. Add salmon, carrots, avocado, and celery, then roll. Open and sprinkle sesame seeds on roller and roll again. Slice the rolls and enjoy.

BR5-49 was discovered at this club on Broadway in Nashville, TN

Tony Brown

I'd call him Tony (Wow) Brown because he is so good-looking. For years the most eligible bachelor on Music Row, he finally got his wings clipped by his beautiful wife, Anastasia. The couple's outlandish wedding reception was attended by everybody who is anybody in show biz, including yours truly.

An ace piano player who once backed Elvis, he became an executive at MCA, where he produced Vince Gill's "When I Call Your Name." Both Tony and Vince have been blessed with a new car to drive ever since.

Once I borrowed $200 from Tony, but when I gave him a check, he tore it up. I was pretty uppity until he explained: "When Elvis died, I was broke. I went to David Briggs and explained my position. David loaned me $1,000. After making some money, I went to repay David. David refused to take my money. He told me he didn't need it, just keep it. And he told me, someday someone who deserves it will need money and you can give it to them. Hazel, you are that somebody. Someday you can help somebody." I believe the Lord smiled that day.

An ace piano player who once backed Elvis…

Tony Brown

Italian Vegetable Soup

- 2 tablespoons olive or vegetable oil
- ½ cup chopped onion
- 1 clove garlic, crushed
- 2 cups zucchini, diced
- 2 cups yellow summer squash, diced
- 1 small green bell pepper, chopped
- ½ cup chopped fresh or 2 tablespoons dried basil leaves
- ½ teaspoon salt
- ¼ teaspoon pepper
- 1 cup uncooked arborio or other short-grain rice (risotto)
- 4 ½ cups vegetable or chicken broth
- 1 28-ounce can whole Italian-style tomatoes, undrained
- grated Parmesan cheese

Heat oil in Dutch oven over medium heat. Cook onion and garlic in oil, stirring occasionally until onion is tender. Stir in zucchini, yellow squash, bell pepper, basil, salt, and pepper. Cook about 8 minutes, stirring frequently, until vegetables are tender.

Stir in rice, broth, and tomatoes, breaking up tomatoes. Heat to boiling over medium-high heat, stirring occasionally; reduce heat to low. Cover and simmer 25–30 minutes or until rice is tender. Serve with cheese.

Makes 6 servings.

Cooking at Tony's house, 2001

Tracy Byrd

A Byrd that can fly, Tracy proved with his first album he was a gold Byrd that turned platinum. With George Jones and Mark Chesnutt, he is one of the Beaumont boys. Once I had this marvelous idea of bottling Beaumont water, because singers all over the world would have it pumped into their homes if they thought they could sing like these guys.

With bragging rights to "Holdin' Heaven" and "The Keeper of the Stars," and hit singles like "Watermelon Crawl" and "I'm From the Country," Tracy decided he needed a change of "homes." Leaving MCA, he titled his first RCA album *It's About Time*. For the first time, Byrd was in the producer's chair alongside guitarist/producer Billy Joe Walker, Jr. Tracy was satisfied with the outcome.

The Byrd who has sold over 5 million records has a heart as big as his home state. The annual Tracy Byrd Homecoming Weekend has raised over $350,000 for charity since 1994. Byrd spends as much time as he can with wife Michelle and children Evee and Logan on their beautiful ranch near Beaumont. Keep drinking that water!

Beer Battered Bass

- 5 pounds of fillets (preferably bass, but I guess any fish will do)
- 1 12-ounce beer
- 2 tablespoons Tabasco® sauce
- 4 tablespoons yellow mustard
- 2 packages Corn-Kits® brand cornbread mix
- 1 cup yellow corn meal
- salt
- pepper
- 1 skillet hot grease OR a deep fryer

Mix beer, Tabasco®, and mustard in a large bowl. Salt and pepper the fillets and coat with beer batter. Put 1 cup of cornmeal and 2 packages of Corn-Kits® in a paper grocery sack. Put battered fillets in sack and shake until fillets are thoroughly coated. Fry in grease until golden brown.

Serve with hushpuppies, french fries, baked beans, and coleslaw, and of course, a cold beer!

NOTE: To truly bring out the flavor of this recipe, you must catch the bass yourself!

The Byrd, who has sold over 5 million records, has a heart as big as his home state.

Shrimp Bread Loaf

- 1 pound shrimp, peeled and deveined
- 1 loaf French bread
- 1 white onion, chopped
- 1 cup shredded Cheddar cheese
- 1 stick butter or margarine
- ½ teaspoon salt
- ½ teaspoon pepper
- ½ teaspoon Tony Chachere's™ Cajun seasoning, or red pepper and paprika

Cut shrimp into small (½") pieces, then sauté in butter and onion over medium heat for about 5 minutes. Cut French bread loaf in half lengthwise. Take the top half and scrape out the center so it looks like a boat. Spread the crumbs on a cookie sheet. Toast the crumbs and the hollow loaf until brown. Combine the crumbs with sautéed shrimp and onions, salt, pepper, and Cajun seasoning, and mix thoroughly. Stuff mixture into the hollowed half of the loaf and spread cheese on top. Bake at 350 degrees for 3–5 minutes or until cheese is melted.

Serve with green salad.

Terri Clark

I met Terri while she was without a record deal, singing "in the round" with other songwriters. Every once in a while I'd run into her someplace on Music Row, and I felt she was country enough to sing a duet with Alan Jackson.

Born in Medicine Bow, Ontario, Canada, Terri embarked for Music City right out of high school. One of her first gigs was singing for tips at Tootsie's. She had no car, so she'd tie her guitar to her hand and ride the trolley to work, get off at 2 a.m., tie the guitar to her hand, and catch a trolley back to her apartment.

After a couple of years, Terri began singing demos and writing songs, scoring big with "Better Things To Do" and "You're Easy On The Eyes." She's opened for Brooks & Dunn and continues to tour regularly. A fine singer with a fine voice, you can count on Terri Clark to keep it country. She's one girl singer who doesn't need to expose her body to succeed. Terri's recipe comes from "somewhere on the road in Canada," courtesy of Greg Kaczor.

One of her first gigs was singing for tips at Tootsies.

Terri Clark

Truffle-Wrapped Cherries

This is one of my favorite holiday treats, but it is great for any special occasion!

You will need approximately 24 maraschino cherries with stems.

Truffle Mixture

- **⅓ cup whipping cream**
- **2 tablespoons butter**
- **2 tablespoons sugar**
- **4 squares semi-sweet chocolate**

Drain cherries and set aside. Combine cream, butter, and sugar and cook in saucepan on low until smooth. Remove from heat and add chocolate. Stir until melted. Chill mixture until firm enough to handle (3–4 hours or overnight). Wrap each cherry in about 1 tsp. of truffle mixture, then chill until very firm.

Chocolate Coating

- **8 squares of chocolate coating**

Partially melt chocolate over hot water or in microwave (watch carefully if using microwave). Remove from heat and continue stirring until completely melted. Dip cherries in melted chocolate and place on wax paper-lined tray. Chill to set chocolate. Enjoy!

Daniels mastered the fiddle, guitar, mandolin, and banjo.

Charlie Daniels

Besides my sons, Billy and Terry, and myself, Charlie Daniels is one of the few people in Music City who knows the sweat it takes to plant, raise, and harvest a crop of tobacco. North Carolina people made a living using every inch of muscle and every ounce of patience to save that crop. It was the only life we knew.

Daniels mastered the fiddle, guitar, mandolin, and banjo. He played rock and roll and had a song cut by Elvis Presley before moving to Nashville. Daniels played on three Bob Dylan albums, including *Nashville Skyline*, and on records for everyone from Ringo Starr to Tanya Tucker. He formed The Charlie Daniels Band in 1971.

In 1974, Daniels inaugurated the Volunteer Jam as an annual charity. "The Devil Went Down To Georgia" was a top country and pop record in 1973. "In America" became a classic.

Daniels' records continue to sell well. He is in demand for concerts and he continues to tour, but Charlie Daniels is still that country boy. He loves the creators of country music, and I've never met a man who loves his country more.

Charlie Daniels

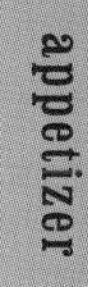

Lemon Pie

Filling

3 egg yolks
1 cup sugar
5 tablespoons cornstarch
juice of 1 lemon (for a tart taste, use 2 lemons)
2 cups boiling water
½ teaspoon salt
2 tablespoons butter

Meringue

4 egg whites
½ teaspoon cream of tartar
8 teaspoons sugar

9" baked pie shell

In the top of a double boiler, beat egg yolks. Combine sugar and cornstarch and add to yolks. Gradually add lemon juice, water, and salt. Stir occasionally and cook until thick. Remove from heat and add butter. Stir and pour the filling into pie shell.

For meringue, beat egg whites. Add sugar and cream of tartar and beat until stiff. Spread on top of filling. Bake at 350-degrees until brown (about 10–12 minutes).

This makes a rich pie and it's good, too!

Makes 8 servings.

He is in demand for concerts and he continues to tour, but Charlie Daniels is still that country boy. He loves the creators of Country Music, and I've never met a man who loves his country more.

Right from the get-go, I fell in love...

Diamond Rio

Diamond Rio is Marty Roe, Jimmy Olander, Dana Williams, Brian Prout, Dan Truman, and Gene Johnson.

Right from the get-go, I fell in love with this handsome bunch of musicians who have given us such smash hits as "One More Day" and "Unbelievable." How could I not?

The most awarded group in country music, individually and collectively, this is the best all-around band in the business. Olander's guitar work, Williams' bass playing, Prout's drumming, Johnson's mandolin playing, Truman's keyboard expertise, and Roe's vocals and acoustic guitar are what you see on the road in concert and what you hear on their records. Yep, they all do all the instrumentation in the recording studio. No other band in country music can boast this claim.

With their many awards, gold and platinum records, accolades and hits, the career highlight for Diamond Rio came when they joined the Grand Ole Opry in 1998. I shall never forget seeing tears stream down Marty Roe's face; Dana Williams, nephew of the Opry's Osborne Brothers, was totally dazed.

I'm proud Diamond Rio wanted to be included in my cookbook.

Devilish Love Bar

Marty Roe of Diamond Rio

This is the cake that Marty and brother Scott always request their mom to make (without nuts) for their birthdays. It is a family birthday tradition!

1 cup water
2 sticks margarine (1 cup)
¼ cup cocoa
2 cups flour
2 cups sugar
1 teaspoon baking soda
2 teaspoons vanilla
2 eggs, beaten
½ cup buttermilk

In a small saucepan, bring water, margarine, and cocoa to a boil. Combine remaining ingredients. Pour hot mixture into remaining ingredients. Grease and flour a 12"x15" sheet pan. Pour batter into sheet pan and bake in 350 degree oven until set (about 20 minutes).

Fudge Icing

½ cup buttermilk
1 stick margarine
½ cup cocoa
1 1-pound box confectioner's sugar
finely chopped nuts sprinkled on top (optional)

Bring milk and margarine to a boil. Add the remaining ingredients and blend with a mixer. Pour over hot cake and cut into bars when cool.

The most awarded group in country music, individually and collectively, this is the best all-around band in the business.

White Chili

Jimmy Olander of Diamond Rio

This is a favorite "once in a while" treat for Jimmy and Claudia Olander that they also like to serve at parties. They give the dish a "high five" for its healthy qualities, too!

1 pound white beans, soaked overnight and drained
6 cups chicken broth
1 tablespoon minced garlic
2 medium onions, chopped
3 teaspoons oil
2 4-ounce cans chopped green chilies
2 teaspoons ground cumin
1½ teaspoons ground oregano
¼ teaspoon cayenne pepper
4 cups cooked chicken breast, diced
3 cups Monterey Jack cheese (optional garnish)

Combine white beans, chicken broth, minced garlic, and 1 of the chopped onions in a large pot. Bring to a boil, then reduce heat and simmer. Cover and simmer for 2 hours. While beans are cooking, sauté remaining onion in oil, add the chicken, cumin, oregano, and cayenne pepper. Add chicken mixture to the beans after the 2 hours. Add the chilies and simmer for 1 hour more.

May also serve with rice, fruit, veggies, bread, or tortillas!

Makes 8–10 servings.

Joe Diffie

One thing's for sure: you'll never mistake Joe Diffie for a pop singer. Traditional Diffie played gospel and bluegrass, worked the Texas oilfields, and sweated in a foundry in hometown Duncan, Oklahoma, where he settled into performing with an aunt and his sister.

Moving to Nashville in the late 1980's, Joe worked at Gibson Guitars, by night writing songs and demoing for other songwriters, which led to his record deal on Epic. His first single, "Home," went to number one in 1990, proving that tradition always pays off. His signature song is "If The Devil Danced (In Empty Pockets)," but my favorite is "Pickup Man." Hit songs, awards, and gold records prompted the Grand Ole Opry to make him a member in 1993.

Diffie's son Tyler has Down Syndrome, which inspired the singer to host an annual benefit for First Steps, the school Tyler attends. Joe was brought to tears when he was surprised with the 1999 Humanitarian Award by the Country Radio Broadcasters (CRB). He's a regular Joe, and these days the singer is happier than he's ever been with his beautiful wife, Teresa.

Moving to Nashville in the late 1980's, Joe worked at Gibson Guitars, by night writing songs and demoing for other songwriters, which led to his record deal on Epic.

Joe Diffie

Chili Dogs

LaVerna "Grandma" Diffie

- 1 package all beef wieners
- 1 package hot dog buns
- mustard
- 1 small onion, chopped
- seasoned salt
- 1 can chili without beans
- 5-6 ounces shredded Cheddar cheese

Turn broiler to low setting. In large saucepan, cover wieners with water and bring to a boil. Cook at steady boil for 2 minutes. In small saucepan, cook chili over low heat. Stir periodically. While wieners and chili are heating, spread mustard evenly onto hot dog buns. Place hot dog buns in two rows in a 9"x13" pan. Put cooked wieners into hot dog buns. Spread chopped onion evenly over each hot dog. Sprinkle seasoned salt generously over hot dogs (this is what gives the hotdogs a wonderfully unique taste). Spoon heated chili evenly over hot dogs. Sprinkle cheese over hot dogs.

Cook for 2–3 minutes under low broil or until cheese is melted and buns are dark golden brown.

Makes 4–6 servings.

Sara Evans

When Sara Evans hit town, Harlan Howard took her to Renee Bell at BMG Records. Bell fell in love with the way the country girl from Missouri sang and signed her to a label deal. I never saw an artist who loved to sing more than Sara.

Her first album, titled *Three Chords and the Truth*, from a song she co-wrote, was a critic's dream. I loved that CD. Her second album, *No Place That Far*, contained a co-written single of the same title, her first number-one hit.

Then Sara had baby Avery. Totally in love with Avery, she took him everywhere she went, and for a time it seemed Sara was more into motherhood than her career. Luckily, she found a way to balance both. Evans discovered through the Scriptures a way to lose weight following Avery's birth and slimmed down to model proportions.

Her third album included her second number-one single, "Born To Fly," also the CD title. Sara and husband Craig have a new home in Brentwood, Tennessee. And Sara actually does cook!

Sara Evans

I never saw an artist who loved to sing more than Sara.

Corn & Macaroni Bake

Granny's recipe

1 can whole grain corn (do not drain)
1 can cream style corn
1 stick melted butter
1 cup cubed Cheddar cheese
1 cup macaroni, uncooked

Pour both cans of corn into a greased 9"x13" baking dish. Add butter, Cheddar cheese, and uncooked macaroni. Mix and bake at 350 degrees for 20 minutes. Remove from oven and stir. Return to oven for 10 minutes or until bubbly and set.

Makes 8–10 servings.

Pete Fisher

Pete keeps up with charts and knows who's hot and who's not.

Hard-working and loyal best describe Pete Fisher, general manager of the Grand Ole Opry.

Pete books the Opry every week. He keeps up with charts and knows who's hot and who's not. He strives to get those artists, in order to fill the house every Friday and Saturday night.

Fisher has chosen three great new Opry members: Pam Tillis, Ralph Stanley, and Brad Paisley. I've seen him stand in the wings and watch each and every act, carefully measuring applause. Pete strives to keep the audience well entertained. During the Opry shows and *Backstage at the Opry*, he is on top of every move made onstage. He is not there to "goose somebody" or poke fun at someone. He's on duty, taking care of business.

To me, the Grand Ole Opry is country music. I've loved the Opry all my life. I go quite often or watch it on TV or listen to it on the radio. It's a wonderful, hallowed institution that I hope and pray will stand forever. I'm glad Pete is taking care of those singers and musicians and the Opry.

Pete Fisher

Hard-working and loyal best describe Pete Fisher, general manager of the Grand Ole Opry.

Backstage at the Opry, 2001

Autumn Soup

1 pound ground beef
1 cup chopped onion
4 cups water
1 cup celery, diced
1 cup potatoes, cubed and pared
1 teaspoon bottled brown bouquet sauce
⅛ teaspoon basil
1 cup cut carrots
2 teaspoons salt
1 bay leaf
6 tomatoes, chopped, or 1 28-ounce can whole tomatoes*

In large saucepan, cook and stir meat until brown. Drain off fat. Cook and stir onions with meat until onions are tender, about 5 minutes. Stir in remaining ingredients (except tomatoes) and heat to boiling. Reduce heat, cover and simmer 20 minutes. Add tomatoes, cover and simmer 10 minutes longer or until vegetables are tender. (Remove bay leaf before serving.)

*If using 1 can of tomatoes, reduce water to 3 cups.

Makes 6 servings.

At home with the Gala

Joe & Phran Galante

I met Joe Galante when Waylon Jennings was hot as a firecracker—lit on both ends.

Joe was the finance guy at RCA. He'd walk out the back door of their old offices over to Glaser Sound Studio, home to Waylon Jennings and Tompall Glaser.

Here, the New York-born, bred, and trained executive was born again at the altar of Waylon Jennings. Joe's life changed in the twinkling of a guitar chord. When he learned to love the music with his heart, he became a new man and an adopted child of the South.

Galante signed Alabama and Keith Whitley—even attending AA with Whitley so he could understand alcoholism. He also signed Clint Black, The Judds, K.T. Oslin, Lonestar, Kenny Chesney, Lorrie Morgan, and young Andy Griggs.

Joe's wife, Phran, worked at RCA/Nashville following a stint at Chrysalis in New York. At Arista, she helped launch Alan Jackson, Lee Roy Parnell, Diamond Rio, and others.

Ten "glorious" years ago (says Phran) the Brooklyn-born army brat became Mrs. Galante, a role that fits her like a glove.

Joe's life changed in the twinkling of a guitar chord.

Joe & Phran Galante

Purée of Pumpkin Soup

- 4 tablespoons (½ stick) margarine
- 1 large onion, chopped
- 1 medium leek, white part only, chopped
- 1 pound canned pumpkin purée
- 4 cups chicken broth
- 1 teaspoon salt
- ½ teaspoon curry powder
- ¼ teaspoon ground nutmeg
- ¼ teaspoon ground white pepper
- ¼ teaspoon ground ginger
- 1 bay leaf
- 1 cup skim milk

In a medium soup pot, melt margarine. Sauté onion and leek, stirring occasionally, until soft. Stir in pumpkin, chicken broth, salt, spices, and bay leaf. Bring to a boil. Lower heat and simmer, uncovered for 15 minutes, stirring occasionally. Remove the bay leaf. Allow to cool. Purée the mixture in batches in blender or food processor for a smooth texture.

At this point, soup may be refrigerated for 2 days or frozen.

Return to soup pot. Add skim milk and cook over moderate heat, stirring occasionally, until heated through. Adjust seasonings.

Makes 6–8 servings.

Vince Gill

Vince Gill's heart is only exceeded in size by his talent. He plays virtually every instrument that's crossed the stage of the Grand Ole Opry—and he's the show's biggest booster. If he isn't on the road, he is at the Opry, something he feels he owes that hallowed stage, its rich history, and the audience.

Oklahoma-born, Vince was with Pure Prairie League and toured with Rodney Crowell and Rosanne Cash. The hauntingly beautiful "When I Call Your Name" took him to the top of the charts and into the hearts of country fans, as did "Go Rest High On That Mountain."

Vince has won more Grammy and CMA awards than anyone else in country music. One of the most loved people on the country music scene, Gill's non-stop charity work is legendary, and he does it as quietly as possible.

Gill used to call himself "a golfer who likes to sing for a living." But since marrying the love of his life in 2000, singer Amy Grant, golf has become secondary. His new-found happiness is so obvious, it makes me feel good to see his face.

At Vince's manager's office, 2001

Vince Gill

White Chocolate Cake

- 1 18.25-ounce box Duncan Hines® Moist Deluxe® Butter Recipe Golden cake mix
- 1 3.4-ounce box vanilla instant pudding (not sugar-free)
- ½ cup sugar
- ⅔ cup cooking oil
- ½ cup water
- 4 eggs
- ½ pint sour cream
- 1 6-ounce package white chocolate chips

Preheat oven to 350 degrees. Grease and lightly flour 2 4½"x8½" loaf pans. Combine cake mix, pudding mix, sugar, oil, water, and eggs in a large bowl. Beat at medium speed with electric mixer for two minutes. Fold in sour cream and white chocolate chips. Bake for 45–50 minutes. Cool in pans for 25 minutes. Cool completely before slicing.

Makes 2 loaves.

Note: You can use chocolate cake mix, chocolate instant pudding, and chocolate chips if you like chocolate, or substitute any flavor cake mix, instant pudding, and chips.

Gill used to call himself "a golfer who likes to sing for a living."

I look for big things from this young man.

Andy Griggs

Cooking at the recording studio, 2001

I wanted Andy Griggs in my cookbook for several reasons.

First, the nice-guy singer favors Brad Pitt—only Andy is better looking. Second, his wife, Stephanie, is the daughter of Jerry Sullivan and sister to Tammy Sullivan, so he's related to that wonderful gospel bluegrass duo from Mississippi. Third, I love the way he sings tunes like "You Won't Ever Be Lonely" and "She's More." Fourth, as a huge fan of real country music—from Bill Monroe to Hank Williams to Waylon Jennings—Griggs has been raised on the best. Last, Griggs knows exactly how to wear his britches—and that's a biggie with all of us young ladies.

The Louisiana singer and songwriter has topped the charts a couple of times with self-penned tunes and has had a couple of top-five singles. His debut album is certified gold. I look for big things from this young man. An outdoorsman, he loves to hunt and fish when he gets precious time off the road. You can tell he's that kind of guy from his duck and seafood recipes.

Seafood Pie

1 9" pie shell
2 tablespoons margarine
¼ cup green bell pepper, chopped
¼ cup green onions, chopped
¼ cup celery, chopped
1 3-ounce can of mushrooms
½ pound lump crabmeat
½ pound shrimp, boiled and peeled
1 cup shredded Cheddar cheese
½ cup fresh grated Parmesan cheese
1 tablespoon lemon juice
5 dashes Tabasco®
1 egg, beaten
¼ cup mayonnaise
Tony Chachere's™ Creole seasoning
¼ cup slivered almonds

Partially bake pie shell at 400 degrees for 5–7 minutes. Remove from oven. Lower heat to 350 degrees. Melt margarine in a large skillet and sauté bell pepper, onions, celery, and mushrooms until tender. Add crabmeat, shrimp, ¾ cup Cheddar cheese, Parmesan cheese, lemon juice, hot pepper sauce, egg, and mayonnaise, stirring well until moist. Add Tony Chachere's™ creole seasoning. Remove from heat and drain excess liquid. Spoon into pie shell and bake for about 20 minutes. Top with almonds and remaining cheese. Bake another 10 minutes.

Makes 6 servings.

Hot Tamale Pie

2 pounds ground beef
2 tablespoons oil
2 onions, chopped
1 clove garlic, minced
1 large green bell pepper
1 cup celery, chopped
1 6-ounce can tomato paste
1-2 tsp. Tony Chachere's™ creole seasoning
Worcestershire sauce
Tabasco® to taste
2 tablespoons chili powder
1 cup whole kernel corn
1 teaspoon salt
3 cups water
1 cup cornmeal

In a deep 12" skillet, fry ground beef in oil. Skim oil from meat and reserve for cornmeal mixture. Add chopped vegetables and sauté 5 minutes. Add tomato paste, Tony Chachere's™ seasoning, 5–6 shakes of Worcestershire, Tabasco® to taste, chili powder, salt, and corn. Cook an additional 5 minutes. Add 1 cup of water and simmer for 1 hour.

In another container, mix cornmeal with cold water. Add oil from top of meat. Season with Tony Chachere's™, Worcestershire, and Tabasco® to taste. Cook 20 minutes and combine with meat mixture. Add a little more Tony's™ to taste.

Place in a 9"x13"x2"casserole dish. Immerse casserole in a larger glass baking dish with water (to prevent burning). Bake for 2 hours at 350 degrees.

Makes 8 servings.

Griggs knows exactly how to wear his britches—and that's a biggie with all of us young ladies.

John Hartford

St. Louis-bred John Hartford was working on a riverboat at age 10, and at 13 was playing banjo.

In Nashville in the mid-1960's, he hung out with fellow songwriters Mickey Newberry and Kris Kristofferson, and soon his "Gentle On My Mind," as recorded by Glen Campbell, made him a household word. Hartford turned down the chance to star in his own television detective series, choosing to write for and appear on *The Smothers Brothers Comedy Hour* and later the *Glen Campbell Goodtime Hour.*

Turning his back on California, he returned to St. Louis and earned his riverboat pilot's license. In Nashville he recorded several delightful albums. Hartford married one of my best friends, Marie Barrett, 20 years ago on the banks of the Cumberland River, where they live today.

He's battled cancer for years, but John Hartford is never too sick to play a tune. He's a singer, songwriter, riverboat captain, author, womper-stomper (dances on a sheet of plywood as he plays and sings), and musician who plays banjo, fiddle, dobro, and guitar. The man loves music more than anybody I have ever met.

He's a singer, songwriter, riverboat captain, author, womper-stomper (dancing as he sings and plays a sheet of plywood), banjo, fiddle, guitar, and dobro player.

John Hartford

Spinach Salad

1 large bunch spinach
1 11-ounce can mandarin oranges, drained
1 bunch green onions, cut into small pieces
8 slices bacon, cooked and crumbled

Dressing

½ cup olive oil
¼ cup balsamic vinegar
¼ cup sugar
¼ cup ketchup

In a salad bowl, combine spinach, mandarin oranges, green onions, and crumbled bacon. In a small bowl, combine dressing ingredients and mix well. Just before serving, toss dressing with salad greens.

Makes 4–6 servings.

Crunchy Chicken Crescents

3 cups chopped, cooked chicken
6 ounces cream cheese with chives
2 tablespoons butter
1 8-count package crescent dinner rolls, separated
1 cup seasoned stuffing mix
¾ cup melted butter

Cream 2 tablespoons butter and cream cheese with chives. Add chopped chicken and mix well. Spoon ¼ cup chicken mixture onto each roll. Roll dough to enclose filling. Seal. Dip rolls into ¾ cup melted butter. Coat in stuffing mix. Place on baking dish. Bake at 375 degrees for 20 minutes.

Alan Jackson

Alan Jackson proudly carries the traditional flag. He loves George Jones just like I do. His favorite song is "He Stopped Loving Her Today," and so is mine.

I recall the time at Fan Fair when Alan sang Gene Watson's "Farewell Party," and I cried backstage like a baby. That, friends, is country: music you feel with your heart that goes on and lives forever.

I wasn't surprised when Alan sent a recipe. That country boy can sop gravy, eat fried potatoes and fried chicken with the best, and likes his sainted mama's pies and cakes.

Winning CMA's Entertainer of the Year award in 1995 was a career highlight for Jackson, but he says having "Chattahoochee" win the 1993 Video and Single of the Year award and 1994 Song of the Year honors were also nice. The way he loved and honored his parents made me know Alan was a good man. It sure hurt him when he lost his dad.

If you've never seen the 6'4", good-looking Jackson sing, do yourself a favor—go, see, enjoy.

Country Fried Steak with Onion Gravy

Alan Jackson

- 1 pound cubed steak
- ½ teaspoon meat tenderizer
- ½ teaspoon salt
- 2¼ tablespoons flour
- ½ cup cooking oil
- ¼ cup chopped onion
- 1½ cups water

Sprinkle steak with meat tenderizer and salt. Dredge steaks in ¼ cup of flour. Heat oil in frying pan. When oil is hot, brown steak on both sides. Remove steak from pan. Reduce heat. Stir in 2 tbsp. flour and dash of salt. Brown flour. Add about 1½ cups water. Return steak to pan. Add chopped onions. Cover. Simmer on low heat 20–30 minutes until meat is tender. If gravy is too thick, add more water to make gravy the right consistency. Serve with hot buttermilk biscuits, whipped potatoes, or hashbrowns, and tossed salad.

With me at a #1 Record Party, 1995

Makes 3–4 servings.

I recall the time at Fan Fair when Alan sang Gene Watson's "Farewell Party," and I cried backstage like a baby. That, friends, is country: music you feel with your heart that goes on and lives forever.

"I got to have this boy in my book..."

Robert Earl Keen

I wanted a Texan in my cookbook, so I searched for Robert Earl Keen.

He'd recorded for Arista/Austin and had just signed with Nashville's new hip label, Lost Highway. I'd read that he'd sold out Billy Bob's in Fort Worth, over 5,000 attendance, and was not surprised. But he also sold out Fillmore West in San Francisco the next week! I learned he sells out venues in Knoxville, Winston-Salem, Raleigh, and wherever he performs.

"I got to have this boy in my book," I thought, and started making calls to Texas—two or three daily. Come to find out, Robert Earl Keen was appearing at 328 Performance Hall in Music City. My friend Kevin Lane drove me there, and as we approached the door a line was spilling out onto the sidewalk and snaking down the street, mostly guys 25 and under.

The act that I thought was mostly a Texas act sold out in Music Town, thanks to hits like "Merry Christmas From The Family." College-age kids by the score sang along with every song. After four encores, past the midnight hour, I had this photo taken with Robert Earl.

Robert Earl Keen

After his Music City concert, 2001

I wanted a Texan in my cookbook, so I searched for Robert Earl Keen.

Smokin' Armadillo

1 Texas armadillo
brisket rub
foil

Take one armadillo, sprinkle with brisket rub, wrap in foil, smoke over low heat for 12 hours. Unwrap and serve at a wild game dinner.

The Kinleys

I used to see the Kinley twins waiting tables at Logan's.

I used to see the Kinley twins down at Rivergate, north of Nashville, waiting tables at Logan's, way back when both had identical long blonde hair and identical lips of red, each eyelash mascara-ed the same, and each girl laughing the same infectious laugh. The twosome would show up around Music Row and nobody knew Jennifer from Heather.

Their debut Sony album, *Just Between You and Me,* made quite a splash for the Philadelphia natives. In 1998, they received a Grammy nomination for Best Country Performance by a Duo/Group, and were named Best Duo/Group by the Academy of Country Music.

Their first album went gold and is headed for platinum. The girls scored a hit with the inspirational "Somebody's Out There Watching" from the *Touched By An Angel* soundtrack, and the song was also included on the girls' second CD, *The Kinleys II.*

Bloodline harmonies cannot be matched. Since the twins each took a giant step in 2000 and got married, it's the first time in 30 years they do not have the same last name. And that's the spin on the twins.

Bloodline harmonies cannot be matched.

The Kinleys

Chicken Wrap

The filling can be made ahead of time and kept refrigerated until ready to wrap.

- **¼ cup chopped walnuts**
- **1 teaspoon olive oil**
- **¾ pound boneless, skinless chicken breasts, cut into 1-inch cubes**
- **½ teaspoon kosher salt (if using table salt, decrease the amount by half)**
- **¼ teaspoon pepper**
- **¼ cup firmly packed crumbled Roquefort cheese**
- **¼ cup blue cheese dressing**
- **⅓ cup dried cherries**
- **¼ cup celery, finely chopped**
- **½ cup firmly packed arugula, chopped**
- **2 10" or 11" flour tortillas (flavored tortilla suggestion: spinach)**

Preheat oven to 350 degrees. Spread walnuts on a baking sheet. Bake until walnuts become aromatic and appear shiny from the oils being released (about 10 minutes). Remove from oven and let cool. Heat olive oil in a large non-stick skillet over high heat. Add chicken. Season with ½ teaspoon kosher salt and ¼ teaspoon pepper. Cook thoroughly, 3–5 minutes, stirring to brown all sides. Let cool. Mix together Roquefort cheese, blue cheese dressing, cherries, and celery. Add chicken. At this point, filling can be refrigerated and finished later if desired. Toss arugula and walnuts into chicken mixture. Divide among tortillas and wrap.

Makes 2 servings.

Chris LeDoux

Chris LeDoux's background sounds like a movie.

Chris LeDoux's background sounds like a movie. He entered his first rodeo at 14, and won the Wyoming State Championship and the Intercollegiate National Bareback Championship before turning professional in 1970. He won the World Championship Bareback Rider buckle before hanging up his spurs in 1980.

During college, LeDoux began writing rodeo songs. In 20 years, he recorded 22 albums of old cowboy songs and more than 100 songs he'd written. Garth Brooks paid homage to LeDoux, his hero, in "Much Too Young (To Feel This Damn Old)," and the two became friends. LeDoux signed with Capitol Records and Garth sang with him on the title cut of his album *Whatcha Gonna Do With a Cowboy.*

LeDoux is in love with his wife and five children. He became deathly ill with a deadly liver disease, and the Country Music and rodeo worlds prayed for a miracle. According to LeDoux's fan club, Garth Brooks did more—he offered to donate part of his liver, only to discover his liver did not match. Fortunately, a compatible donor was discovered and Chris's life was saved.

He won the World Championship Bareback Rider buckle before hanging up his spurs in 1980.

Chili

2 pounds hamburger (ground beef)
1 clove garlic, chopped
1 green bell pepper, chopped
½ cup onion, chopped
1 74-ounce can tomato sauce
1 bay leaf
2-3 tablespoons chili powder
1-2 16-ounce cans of chili beans

Fry hamburger, garlic, green pepper, and onion on medium heat until meat is browned. Add tomato sauce, bay leaf, chili powder, and beans. Cook on low for 30 minutes to one hour. (Remove bay leaf before serving.)

Makes 6–8 servings.

Stew

Ingredients: Whatever you have left in your refrigerator, such as carrots, celery, onions, potatoes, cabbage, cauliflower, beef and fat, broccoli, etc. Personally, I like the following:

4-6 potatoes
2-4 carrots
½ cup onion, chopped
1 clove garlic, minced
3-4 ribs celery, chopped
1 28-ounce can tomatoes
1 T-bone or something good (along with the fat, bone and all), cut in chunks
water (enough to boil the vegetables—about 3 cups)
salt and pepper

If the meat is not already cooked, brown in a large pot. Add water and bring to a boil. Add vegetables and simmer until tender. Add the other ingredients and cook until it tastes good enough to eat.

Patty Loveless

My son Billy and I love to hear Patty Loveless sing. Her crystal-clear mountain vocals give chill bumps to chill bumps.

Born on the Kentucky side of the mountain that gave birth to Ricky Skaggs, Keith Whitley, Larry Cordle, the Osborne Brothers, Loretta Lynn, the Judds, Tom T. Hall, and Dwight Yoakam, Patty grew up with the mournful songs of coal miners' widows in Pikeville, Kentucky.

Her first MCA album in 1985 was co-produced by Emory Gordy, Jr., who became her husband. Loveless will be remembered for her incredible harmony with Vince Gill on "When I Call Your Name." Her signature single, "Blame It On Your Heart," was her first number-one on Epic, taken from her certified-gold CD, *Only What I Feel.* I also love "Chains." Named the CMA's Female Vocalist in 1996, Patty, having recovered from vocal chord surgery, was on an emotional high until her sister's death, followed shortly by her husband Emory Gordy's close call after pancreatic surgery.

Patty and Emory have a Music City apartment and a dream home in the mountains of Georgia near Gordy's daughter and grandchild.

Her crystal-clear mountain vocals give chill bumps to chill bumps.

Patty Loveless

Cauliflower & Potatoes

I serve this as a side dish with roasted chicken. It's a favorite in our house. Enjoy!

- **2 medium potatoes, boiled in skins (day old cooked potatoes are good to use—not too done, though)**
- **1 small head cauliflower**
- **4 tablespoons cooking oil (vegetable or canola)**
- **1½ teaspoon whole cumin seeds**
- **½ teaspoon ground coriander seeds**
- **¼ teaspoon ground turmeric**
- **¼ teaspoon cayenne pepper**
- **1 teaspoon salt**
- **freshly ground black pepper**

Roast ½ teaspoon whole cumin seeds in a hot, dry skillet for 4–6 seconds to brown. Remove from skillet, grind, and set aside. Remove skins of cooled potatoes and cut into 1" cubes. Break cauliflower into chunky flowerets, about 1½" long. Soak flowerets in a bowl of water for 30 minutes. Drain and dry off excess water with paper towel. Heat oil in a large non-stick frying pan over medium heat. When oil is hot, add remaining whole cumin seeds and let sizzle for a few seconds. Add cauliflower and stir for approximately 2 minutes, browning in spots. Cover and simmer for 4–6 minutes until cauliflower is slightly done with a hint of crispness. Add diced potatoes and remaining spices. Stir lightly to mix and cook uncovered on low heat for 3–4 minutes.

Makes 4 servings.

Martina McBride

Martina McBride is living proof a country singer can also be a lady.

The Ryman Auditorium, Nashville, TN

The prettiest eyes in showbiz belong to Martina McBride. When she looks at you, you feel like she sees clear into your soul.

Her first paying gig in Music Town was selling merchandise for the Garth Brooks Tour. Soon, she was opening shows for Brooks. Now the whole world loves her for hits like "My Baby Loves Me" and her incredible version of "Independence Day."

Her husband John, Garth's former sound man, and their daughters, Delaney and Emma, are the loves of Martina's life. Delaney started school this year, so Martina works mostly weekends so she can drive her daughter to school, bake cookies, be a room mother, and attend PTO meetings.

I saw the gleam in her eyes when she first told me she was pregnant with Delaney. I stood in the wings as she brushed off her dad's jacket, straightened his tie, and toted his guitar backstage so he could make his Opry debut with her. I've watched her and John bring both girls to the Opry when Martina performs. Martina McBride is living proof a country singer can also be a lady.

Curried Chicken Soup

1 cup long grain white rice
1 cup onion, diced
1 cup carrot, diced
½ cup butter
8 cups chicken broth
3-4 chicken breast halves, cooked and diced (I always bake mine, covered with a can of chicken broth, covered with tin foil, at 350 degrees for about an hour and a half, or until done and tender)
3 teaspoons curry powder
½ teaspoon turmeric
½ cup all-purpose flour
1 cup milk
1 cup half-and-half
1 cup frozen peas, thawed

(You can add more peas and carrots than it calls for. Add a little broth or water to keep it from becoming too thick, but not too much. It is supposed to have a thick, hearty consistency.) Sauté rice, onion, and carrot in butter for 5 minutes. Add chicken broth, chicken, turmeric, and curry powder. Cover and simmer until rice is cooked, about 20 minutes. Blend flour into milk and gradually stir into soup until mixture thickens. Just before serving, stir in half-and-half and peas. Heat to serving temperature. Good served with crusty French bread.

Makes 8–10 servings.

When she looks at you, you feel like she sees clear into your soul.

Corn Corn Bread

½ cup all-purpose flour
1¼ cups yellow cornmeal
¾ cup granulated sugar
½ teaspoon baking powder
½ teaspoon baking soda
½ teaspoon salt
2 large eggs
½ cup vegetable oil
½ cup milk
½ cup buttermilk
1 cup fresh corn, cooked (I use frozen corn)

Preheat oven to 350 degrees. Grease a 9"x5"x3" loaf pan and dust with cornmeal. In a large bowl, combine flour, cornmeal, sugar, baking powder, baking soda, and salt. Whisk together eggs, oil, milk, and buttermilk in a medium bowl. Add egg mixture to dry ingredients, stirring until just moistened. Fold corn into batter. Pour into prepared pan and bake for 15 minutes. Reduce heat to 325 degrees and continue baking until a wooden toothpick inserted in the center comes out clean, about 30–45 additional minutes. Cool on a wire rack for 30 minutes before removing from pan.

Reba McEntire

From the time Reba McEntire could tote a bucket, the Chokie, Oklahoma, ranch kid was raking hay, feeding cattle, and riding horses.

Her first number-one song, "Can't Even Get the Blues," was in 1982. But such tunes as "Is There Life Out There" and my favorite, "Somebody Should Leave," catapulted her to superstardom. One of the top-selling female recording artists in country music, she's also one of the hardest workers. She's had hit after hit and won virtually every award, including Entertainer of the Year.

The redhead also scored big on Broadway as the lead in *Annie Get Your Gun.* New York media gave Reba rave reviews, but shoot, I wasn't surprised. I could've told them that they were writing about a gal who used to hold the bucket while her daddy castrated the bull calves back home in Chokie. Then she'd take the bucket to the house where her mama would fry 'em up for supper. It's called making do, out in the country.

When she isn't out of town, Reba and her manager/husband, Narvel Blackstock, reside comfortably in Wilson County with their son, Shelby.

One of the top-selling female recording artists in country music, she's also one of the hardest workers.

Reba McEntire

Yogurt Chicken

1 cup non-fat plain yogurt
½ cup fresh lemon juice
1 teaspoon curry powder
1 teaspoon cumin
1 teaspoon cinnamon
1-2 garlic cloves, minced
4 large boneless chicken breast halves

In a small bowl, combine all ingredients except chicken and mix well. Score top of chicken by making shallow cuts, about ⅛ to ¼" deep. Place chicken in a zip-top plastic bag and add yogurt mixture. Turn bag until chicken is coated. Let stand at room temperature for 15 minutes. Spray broiler pan with non-stick cooking spray. Place chicken on sprayed pan; brush with yogurt mixture. Broil 6" from heat for 6–8 minutes. Turn chicken; brush with yogurt mixture. Broil an additional 7–9 minutes or until chicken is fork tender and juices run clear. Discard any remaining yogurt mixture.

Makes 4 servings.

Jo Dee Messina

She won CMA's Horizon Award...

Born near Boston, red-headed fireball Jo Dee sparkles. But there was a time when she felt like just a face in the crowd.

Jo Dee Messina came to Music Town to become a singer. Broken promises came easy and often, but she didn't give up, and found a gig singing at a club where Byron Gallimore heard her and was blown away. Months later, Messina thought, "What could I lose?" and made an appointment. Upon arrival at Gallimore's office, she met another wannabe named Tim McGraw, who invited Messina to Fan Fair. She went, and, not knowing it wasn't kosher, got in a Curb exec's face and explained her plight. 'Nuff said. Before you knew it, country fans were hearing "I'm Alright" and "Bye Bye."

Jo Dee's "That's The Way" hung for four weeks at number one—a first for a woman! She won CMA's Horizon Award, ACM's Top New Female award, and a 1999 Grammy nomination. In February 2001, Messina kicked off her first headline tour. Engaged to road manager Don Muzquiz, she has 5 carats to prove it. Ahead is where she's headed.

Magic Bars

Jo Dee's mom, Mary, would often make these simple yet delicious treats for parties, church, or social functions. Now, Jo Dee brings these as her contribution to gatherings.

- **½ cup melted butter**
- **1½ cups finely crushed graham crackers**
- **1½ cups coconut**
- **2 cups semi-sweet chocolate**
- **1 14-ounce can sweetened condensed milk**
- **1½ cups chopped walnuts**

Preheat oven to 350 degrees. Combine melted butter and crushed graham crackers. Press mixture into a 9"x13" pan. Layer the last four ingredients on the graham cracker crust in the order listed. Bake for 30 minutes. Let cool and then cut into bars.

Makes 36 pieces.

She won ACM's Top New Female award and a 1999 Grammy nomination.

Favorite Lasagna

Prepare your favorite meat sauce the night before.

- **1 16-ounce box lasagna noodles**
- **1 18-ounce carton ricotta cheese**
- **1 16-ounce carton creamed cottage cheese**
- **½ cup grated Parmesan cheese**
- **2 eggs, beaten**
- **3 teaspoon dried oregano leaves, crushed**
- **½ teaspoon salt**
- **¼ teaspoon pepper**
- **3-4 cups shredded mozzarella cheese**
- **about 6 cups meat sauce**

Prepare lasagna noodles per package directions; let stand in cold water while making cheese filling. Combine ricotta, cottage, and Parmesan cheeses. Add egg, salt, pepper, and oregano and mix well. In a 9"x13" pan, begin layering ingredients, starting with part of the meat sauce, then lasagna noodles, cheese filling, and mozzarella. Repeat layers until you have reached top of pan. Top with another layer of meat sauce.
Bake uncovered in a 350 degree oven for 45 minutes.

Makes 8–10 servings.

Bill Monroe

Fried potatoes were Bill's favorite food. He learned to cook them in the fireplace when he and his Uncle Pen Vandiver, for whom he wrote "Uncle Pen, "were "baching it" in a hilltop cabin overlooking Rosine, Kentucky. Both parents were dead and his brothers and sisters had moved, leaving their teenage brother to fend for himself. Uncle Pen took in the shy, cross-eyed boy.

Bill also learned to love music from Uncle Pen, who played a fiddle. When he joined the Grand Ole Opry in 1939, he changed the sound of music eternally with tunes like "Blue Moon of Kentucky." Eventually the music he developed was called "bluegrass," after his band. From 1945 to 1948, Monroe's Bluegrass Boys were Lester Flatt on guitar, Earl Scruggs on banjo, Chubby Wise on fiddle, Cedric Rainwater on the upright bass, and Monroe on mandolin—considered the definitive bluegrass band by aficionados and scholars to this day.

My sons, Billy and Terry, worked with Bill on his Goodlettsville farm and have marvelous stories to tell about those days when they were teenagers.

I miss Bill more than I've ever missed anyone and I thank God every day that he came into my life and the lives of my two sons.

Me and Bill, 1974

Backstage at CMA Awards, 1972

Fried Potatoes

Peel and wash 5–6 potatoes.
Slice potatoes about ⅛" or less in thickness.
Fill cast iron frying pan ¾" full of potatoes.
Add ½ cup lard and ½ cup water.
Put lid on and let potatoes cook on medium heat until tender.
Stir often from the bottom.
Add salt and pepper.

Fried potatoes were Bill's favorite food. When he cooked fried potatoes, he didn't use a pan with a lid that fit. He'd use a flat lid on an iron skillet. "That's the way my mother did it," Bill remembered. His mother died when Bill was 10.

When Bill learned to fry potatoes himself, he and his Uncle Pen Vandiver, for whom he wrote the song "Uncle Pen," were "baching" in a cabin on a hill overlooking Rosine, Kentucky. Both his parents were dead and his brothers and sisters, all older than Bill, had moved off to Hammond, Indiana, leaving their teenage brother to fend for himself. Uncle Pen took in the shy, cross-eyed boy. His uncle didn't have a cookstove. Bill and Uncle Pen fried potatoes in the fireplace over hot coals and they cooked beans in a pot hanging over the fire. "Late in the evening 'bout sundown, High on the hill and above the town, Uncle Pen played the fiddle Lord how'd ring. You could hear it talk, you could hear it sing."

John Michael Montgomery

When I heard John Michael Montgomery had cut "Life's A Dance," I knew he'd recorded a hit song. Right out of the chute, his first single went to number four. The man does have a knack for choosing hit songs.

The Danville, Kentucky, native was discovered while performing with his brother Eddie and Troy Gentry, who today are recording hits as Montgomery Gentry. His sophomore album, *Kickin' It Up*, went quadruple platinum, and included "I Swear," the most played song on country radio in 1994. His *John Michael Montgomery* CD was another quad-platinum record.

By 2000 he had a beautiful wife, two kids, and a beautiful home in Nicholasville, Kentucky, where he could entertain himself hunting and fishing. Then, out of left field came a tape with a song entitled "The Little Girl." The head of Atlantic Records, Barry Coburn, played me a demo of the song and I about flipped. It was another number one for Montgomery.

The first star who posed with me for the cookbook was John Michael and I'm grateful for that.

The man does have a knack for choosing hit songs.

John Michael Montgomery

Wild Goose with Currant Sauce

1 cooking apple, cut into wedges
1 large orange, unpeeled and cut into wedges
8 pitted prunes, chopped
2 8-pound wild geese, dressed*
2 envelopes dry onion soup mix
2 cups dry red wine
2 cups water
currant sauce

Combine fruit, stir well, and place ½ of the mixture into each goose cavity. Place each goose, breast side up, in an oven cooking bag. Combine soup mix, wine, and water; pour ½ of the mixture into each bag. Seal bag and cut 5–6 slits into each bag, allowing steam to escape. Then put in shallow roasting pan. Bake at 350 degrees for 3–3½ hours. Serve with currant sauce.

*A large, dressed duck can also be used for this recipe.

Currant Sauce

½ cup red currant jelly
¼ cup ketchup
¼ cup port wine
¼ cup Worcestershire sauce
2 tablespoons butter

Combine sauce ingredients and cook over low heat until thoroughly heated.

John and me at a BMI #1 Record Party, 2001

Crock Pot Venison

1 pound venison
2 tablespoons brown sugar
1 teaspoon horseradish
1 tablespoon dehydrated onion
½ cup ketchup
1½ cups water

Cut venison into 1" cubes and place in crockpot. Combine ingredients and pour over meat. Cover and cook on low for 6–8 hours or until tender, stirring several times.

Makes 4–6 servings.

Backstage at the Opry, 2001

Almost 25 years ago, when the Oak Ridge Boys crossed over from gospel music with *Y'all Come Back Saloon,* they quickly became one of country's most popular acts. Their most remembered hits include "Elvira" and "American Made."

Joe Bonsall, Duane Allen, William Lee Golden, and Richard Sterban project a flamboyant image, and their stage show is one of the most entertaining in showbiz, right down to Bonsall's hipness, Allen's three-piece suits, Golden's mountain-man image, and trendy Sterban, who always looks like he's leaped off the pages of GQ.

Bonsall is a successful children's author, and is happily married. Allen and his beautiful wife, Norah Lee, who performs with the Opry's Carole Lee Singers, are doting grandparents of two. Grandfather Golden has released a box set of all his songs. He and his pretty wife of 11 years are expecting their first baby! Sterban has business interests in several minor league baseball teams. He resides in Hendersonville, Tennessee, with his lovely bride of many years.

Count on being royally entertained anytime you attend an Oak Ridge Boys concert.

Old Fashioned Sugar Cookies

1 cup butter
1 cup vegetable oil
1 cup granulated sugar
1 cup powdered sugar
1 teaspoon vanilla
2 eggs
1 teaspoon baking soda
6 cups flour
1 teaspoon cream of tartar
1 teaspoon salt
additional ½ cup granulated sugar to use for finishing

Preheat oven to 375 degrees. Lightly grease a cookie sheet and set aside. In mixing bowl, thoroughly cream butter, oil, and both sugars. Add vanilla and eggs. Sift dry ingredients. Stir into butter mixture and blend. Roll 1 teaspoon of dough into a ball. Roll ball in additional ½ cup granulated sugar and place on greased cookie sheet. Press down lightly on cookie with a glass tumbler or cup that has been dipped in sugar. Flatten with a fork dipped in water. Bake approximately 12 minutes. Remove from cookie sheet and cool on rack.

Makes 10 dozen.

Count on being royally entertained anytime you attend an Oak Ridge Boys concert.

Hatch Show Prints on the walls of a local club, Nashville, T

I've never seen a performer communicate better with an audience than this woman.

K.T. Oslin

One of music's "80's Ladies" was definitely K.T. Oslin. She wrote her songs, went on the road, collected her songwriting royalties, and sat down and counted her money. She had enough to live on if she was careful. And K.T. is careful.

What is she doing? She takes care of her house and her yard. She writes songs. She supports animal rights. She has recorded a new album for RCA that was produced by The Mavericks' Raoul Malo. She does benefits. That sweet girl even buys watermelons and schleps them to the elephants at the retirement sanctuary out in the country near Hohenwald, Tennessee.

I glimpsed her recently and made an attempt to get near her, but people mushroomed between us. K.T. looks great. And if she never performs hits like "Come Next Monday" again in concert, thank God we had her for a while. Her experiences in New York did wonders for her stage presence. I've never seen a performer communicate better with an audience than this woman. Her body language and facial expressions, like her songs, speak volumes.

K.T. Oslin

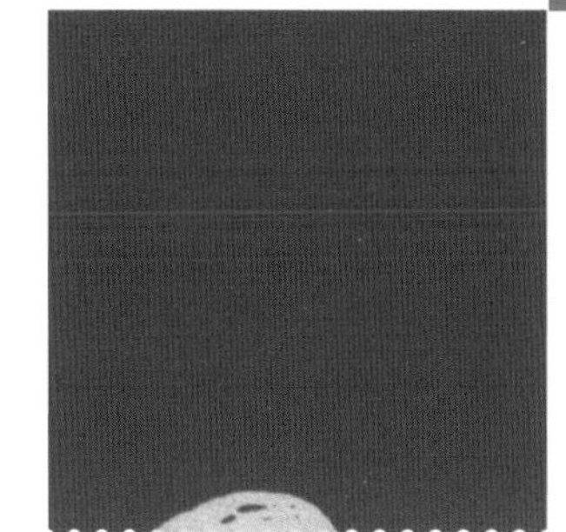

Forty Clove Garlic Chicken

Don't be afraid of the garlic in this recipe. It is delicious and good for you.

1 whole chicken
40 cloves of garlic, separated but not peeled
olive oil (enough to drizzle over the chicken)
¼ teaspoon rosemary
¼ teaspoon sage
½ teaspoon salt
½ teaspoon pepper

Place whole chicken in heavy Dutch oven and drizzle with olive oil. Sprinkle herbs and salt and pepper over chicken. Place garlic cloves all around the chicken. Cover Dutch oven and seal edges with a flour and water mixture (like putty—about 1½ teaspoon flour with 1 teaspoon water). Cook in oven at 350 degrees, according to the weight of the chicken (2 pound chicken, 1½ hours, etc.).

Grill sliced French bread until crunchy and brown. When chicken is done, pop lid off and remove chicken, juices, and garlic. The garlic is spread over the grilled bread and, of course, dipped in the juice.

This dish is best eaten right away. The garlic does get strong if left overnight.

Bon Appétit!

Patti Page

I was a high school senior, maybe all of 16 years old, the first time I saw Patti Page perform. Our graduation class made the traditional senior trip to Washington, D.C., and Patti was performing at Loew's Capitol Theatre.

We sat in the nosebleed section and saw this marvelous woman sing "Tennessee Waltz." She wore a long, white gown and looked fabulously rich to my country girl's eyes. It's no wonder I became smitten by show biz.

Her longstanding career still flourishes. The 71-year-old singer continues to perform simply because she loves to sing. Page records in Music City these days. It was my good fortune to sit by Patti during dinner at the Wild Boar here in Nashville a couple years ago. Believe you me, I was quite the cat's meow when I shared that bit of information with former classmates at our high school reunion. It gave all of us a chance to get naïve and big-eyed all over again. I am honored to include recipes from the kitchen of the great Patti Page.

Her longstanding career still flourishes. The 71-year-old singer continues to perform simply because she loves to sing.

Patti Page

Chicken Patti

- 1 cup soy sauce
- ½ cup A-1® sauce
- 1 10-ounce can Snap-E-Tom®
- 1 cup white wine
- 2 tablespoons Worcestershire sauce
- 1 whole frying chicken (the amount of chicken may be increased as desired in proportion to the amount of sauce used for your taste)

Cut chicken and put in a foil-lined baking dish. Season with garlic powder or salt, as you prefer, and pepper. Pour sauce mixture over chicken. Bake in a 350 degree oven. When sauce cooks down and chicken has browned, turn chicken. Approximate cooking time is 2½ hours, or as long as it takes for sauce to stick to chicken so you may eat it with your fingers.

Enjoy!

Baked Apples with Ginger Snap

- 2-3 21-ounce cans apple pie filling
- 8-10 ginger snaps (or as many as you want)

Empty at least two cans of apple pie filling into oblong baking dish. Crush ginger snaps and sprinkle generously over apples. Bake in 350 degree oven until hot and bubbly—about 30 minutes. Temperature is not crucial.

Fabulous with ham or pork.

Makes 6 servings.

When Brad Paisley took my arm backstage at the CMA Awards 2000 and led me onstage, I introduced the handsome singer as the Savior of Country Music. It caused quite a stir and I'm glad – it was time someone pointed out the young singer's importance.

A songwriter and musician, his award-winning, number-one song about stepfathers, "He Didn't Have To Be," helped story songs resurface on country radio. It also paved the way for his second number-one single, "We Danced," and shoved his gold debut album, "Who Needs Pictures," to solid platinum.

Like a breath of fresh air from the hills, Paisley's affair with radio, fans, the media, and Music Row is incredible. His genuine love for the Grand Ole Opry was rewarded in February 2001, when he became a member of the show—not without tears. The humble star says nothing will ever exceed his Opry induction, the proudest moment of his career. With people like Brad Paisley singing homemade story songs, country music has a healthy future.

Brad and me are kissing friends. Just thought you'd like to know. And isn't he just the cutest thing?

Brad Paisley

Ham Loaf

His mother Sandy's recipe

- 2 pounds processed canned ham loaf
- 1 can bread crumbs
- ½ cup tomato soup
- ½ cup evaporated milk
- 2 eggs (you can substitute Egg Beaters® if you prefer)

Break ham loaf apart and combine with other ingredients. Place in loaf pan (may use 2 pans). Bake, covered with foil, for 1 hour at 350 degrees. Pour off grease after 1 hour.

Topping

- ⅓ cup ketchup
- 3 tablespoons mustard
- 2 tablespoons vinegar
- ½ cup brown sugar

Mix, pour over loaf. Keep portions to add to individual pieces on plate. Bake uncovered, after adding topping, for additional 30 minutes. Serve.

Makes 6–8 servings.

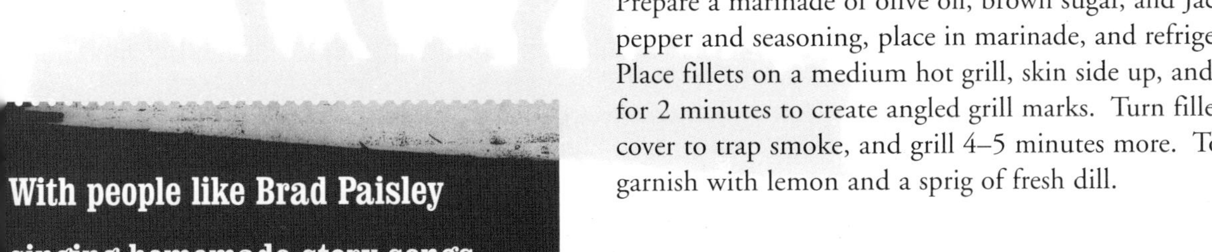

Nashville's new Country Music Hall of Fame

Marinated Grilled Fillet of Salmon

- 4 salmon fillets
- 6 ounces Jack Daniel's® whiskey
- 4 tablespoons brown sugar
- 4 tablespoons olive oil
- blackened seasoning
- pepper to taste

Prepare a marinade of olive oil, brown sugar, and Jack Daniel's®. Sprinkle fillets with pepper and seasoning, place in marinade, and refrigerate for 2–3 hours. Prepare grill. Place fillets on a medium hot grill, skin side up, and grill for 3 minutes. Rotate slightly for 2 minutes to create angled grill marks. Turn fillets over carefully, skin side down, cover to trap smoke, and grill 4–5 minutes more. Top with a pat of seasoned butter; garnish with lemon and a sprig of fresh dill.

Dolly Parton

Dolly Parton is the smartest person ever born in Tennessee.

One of twelve children born to a poor, hard-working couple in the hills of East Tennessee, Dolly began singing on TV as a youngster in Knoxville. After high school, she headed to Nashville, where Porter Wagoner's TV show introduced her to country fans. But it was Dolly's RCA records and her God-given voice that made her a superstar.

In time, Dolly formed her own band, then hosted her own TV show with guests like Linda Ronstadt and Emmylou Harris. Soon, the little blonde with the big bust and bigger dreams, who had sung down-home duets with Wagoner, was getting both pop and country awards. Her self-penned farewell to Wagoner, "I Will Always Love You," went number one several times, including Whitney Houston's soundtrack version for the movie *The Bodyguard*. And tunes like "Jolene" and "9 To 5" have become classics.

Singer, songwriter, musician, TV host, actress, businesswoman — Lordy mercy, Dolly even owns her own theme park, Dollywood, near her mountain home in east Tennessee. Isn't it wonderful the great Dolly Parton wanted to be in my cookbook!

Dolly Parton is the smartest person ever born in Tennessee.

Dolly Parton

Dolly's Country Music Hall of Fame induction, 2000

Islands in the Stream

- **3 eggs, separated**
- **⅔ cup sugar**
- **2 heaping teaspoons flour**
- **1 quart milk**
- **1 teaspoon vanilla**
- **nutmeg (optional)**

Cream egg yolks with sugar and whip until smooth. Add flour and mix well. Scald milk and, when hot enough, add cream mixture. Stir constantly, 20–25 minutes, until it thickens. Remove from heat and add vanilla.

Boil some water (2–3 cups). Whip egg whites and add to water until hardened. Remove with spatula and put on top of cream mixture. Sprinkle with nutmeg. Chill.

Riders in the Sky

I've known Ranger Doug (Doug Greene) since he played bass, while a teen-age college student, for Bill Monroe.

After moving to Twang Town he worked at the Country Music Foundation, wrote a couple of books, played music around town, and eventually realized there was a void in Western music. He learned to yodel, and dreamed of being a modern-day Sons of the Pioneers.

Doug earned an M.A. in English literature. Bass-playing Too Slim (aka Fred) LaBour has a degree in wildlife management, and Woody Paul, the fiddler, has, for Pete's sake, a Ph.D. in plasma physics. (Incidentally, it was Too Slim who, as a student at the University of Michigan, started the rumor that Paul McCartney was dead.)

Too Slim and Woody Paul, like their partner Ranger Doug, are dreamers who love music as much and having a good time. For 23 years they've been making music the cowboy way, fairly well demented onstage, but delivering a clean family show. Kids know and love the Grammy-winning trio for "Woody's Roundup" from Disney's *Toy Story 2.*

Mama Meat's Bean Soup

Compliments of Sidemeat, trail cook for Riders in the Sky

- **1 1-pound bag navy beans**
- **1 ham bone**
- **1 14.5-ounce can tomatoes, diced**
- **1 onion, diced**
- **1 cup celery, diced**
- **1 teaspoon salt**
- **¼ teaspoon pepper**
- **2 bay leaves**
- **½ teaspoon oregano**

Soak navy beans overnight in 8 cups of water. Drain. Place in a Dutch oven with 8 cups of water. (Remember to get the water upstream from the herd!) Add a meaty ham bone, diced tomatoes, diced onion, and some diced celery. Add some salt, pepper, bay leaves, oregano, or whatever. This here's your chance to be creative or else use up what's festering in back of the pantry. Simmer for 2–4 hours, until beans are desired tenderness. Dice the meat, put it back in the soup, and give the bone to your dog (remove bay leaves). Secret of greatness: put about 2 cups of soup in a blender and rile it up 'til it's a cloudy liquid and pour it back in the soup. Let it cook 'til it's the way that suits you. Ummm boy, now that's good eatin'!

Makes 8–10 servings.

For 23 years they've been making music the cowboy way, fairly well demented onstage, but delivering a clean family show.

Sawyer Brown

Sawyer Brown is a really fun group. The band got its start in 1984 by winning $100,000 on the TV show *Star Search*, and has been making good records and putting on good shows ever since.

Lead singer Mark Miller and keyboard player Hobie Hubbard began performing together during high school in Apopka, Florida, and even then Miller was dancing. Bass player Jim Scholten had played in a rock band, met lead guitarist/vocalist Bobby Randall, and together they toured the country. In 1983, their agent convinced them to come to Nashville and make a video. As it turned out, the video was for *Star Search*, where their performance earned them a record deal with Capitol/Curb.

Sawyer Brown has consistently had hit singles and albums during their 17-year reign. The group's first hit was "Step That Step," and their biggest was "Thank God for You." Randall departed in 1992 and Duncan Cameron stepped in. Today, Miller, Hubbard, Scholten, Cameron, and drummer/percussionist Joe Smyth make up the band.

The unusual name? Mark Miller took it from the name of a road near his home between Franklin and Nashville.

Sawyer Brown has consistently had hit singles and albums during its 17-year reign.

Sawyer Brown

Shrimp Kabobs

Mark Miller

- **1⅓ cups soy sauce**
- **⅔ cup lemon juice**
- **1 small onion, minced**
- **1 clove garlic, minced**
- **2½ pounds shrimp, peeled and deveined**
- **12 cherry tomatoes**
- **1 large green bell pepper, cut into 1" squares**

Prepare a marinade with soy sauce, lemon juice, onion, and garlic. Marinate shrimp in refrigerator for approximately 2½ hours. Place shrimp, tomatoes, and green pepper chunks on skewers and broil for 10 minutes, turning several times.

Makes 6 servings.

Chocolate Turbo Cake

Mark & Lisa Miller

- **1 box chocolate devil's food cake mix**
- **1 6-ounce box instant chocolate pudding mix**
- **1 cup oil**
- **½ cup warm water**
- **1 cup sour cream**
- **4 eggs (Lisa only uses 3 eggs)**
- **1 6-ounce bag semi-sweet chocolate morsels (Nestlé® mini morsels)**

In a large mixing bowl, combine cake mix, pudding mix, oil, water, sour cream, and eggs. Beat with an electric mixer on low for 1 minute until combined. Mix for 3 minutes on medium. Fold in chocolate morsels and pour into a well-greased bundt pan. Bake in a pre-heated 350 degree oven for 1 hour. The cake can be served plain, with icing, or dusted with confectioner's sugar.

Makes 10–12 servings.

SHe DAISY

I met the pretty threesome known as SHeDAISY when they were still Kassidy, Kelsi, and Kristyn Osborn, trying to decide on a stage name. They harmonized a capella for me at Lyric Street Records and I could not believe it. They were not traditional country by any stretch of the imagination, but the girls could sing, and they were drop-dead gorgeous, too.

Their first CD, *The Whole SHeBANG,* went platinum, and their 2000 Christmas album, *Brand New Year,* was certified gold. They are itching to perform onstage where they belong, and that wish will obviously soon be granted. Young people love these young ladies. They have a web site and love visiting with their fans, which gives them all the more reason to want to get out there for a meet-and-greet.

The sister with Elvis-black hair who sings lead is Kassidy; the tall, svelte blond is Kristyn, the songwriter; and the sassy redhead is Kelsi, who is married and can cook. We had tons of fun taking pictures for the cookbook at the lovely Brentwood, Tennessee, home of Lyric Street's Senior VP of Promotion & Product Development, Carson Schreiber.

Pre-dinner party festivities, 20(

Peppermint Brownie Sandwiches

- **1 stick (½ cup) butter**
- **⅓ cup cocoa**
- **2 cups sugar**
- **4 eggs**
- **1½ cups flour**
- **2 teaspoon vanilla**
- **1 cup chopped nuts (optional)**

Frosting and Topping

- **2 cups powdered sugar, sifted**
- **¼ cup soft butter**
- **1 tablespoon light cream**
- **1 teaspoon peppermint flavoring**
- **food coloring (optional)**
- **2 squares unsweetened chocolate**
- **2 tablespoon butter**

Blend 1 stick butter, cocoa, and sugar together. Add eggs one at a time. Beat well. Add to above mixture flour, vanilla, and chopped nuts. Bake in greased and floured 9"x13" pan at 350 degrees for 25–30 minutes. Cool completely. Make frosting with first 4 ingredients and spread onto brownies. Let set. Melt chocolate and butter in small pan over low heat. Pour over frosted brownies and spread evenly. Refrigerate to harden. Enjoy!

They were not traditional country by any stretch of the imagination, but the girls could sing, and they were drop-dead gorgeous, too.

Jiffy Bread Sticks

- **1 loaf frozen white bread dough**
- **¼ cup butter or margarine, softened**
- **¼ cup mayonnaise (not salad dressing)**
- **¼ cup grated Parmesan cheese**
- **1 tablespoon parsley flakes**
- **1½ teaspoon garlic salt**
- **sesame seeds to taste (optional)**

Thaw bread dough on greased baking sheet covered with a towel, about 3–4 hours. Make mixture of butter, mayonnaise, cheese, garlic, and parsley. Whip until smooth. Roll bread dough into rectangle shape on baking sheet. Brush dough evenly with mixture. Using a pizza cutter, cut rectangle into strips. Cover dough with towel and let rise until it doubles in size, about 1 hour. Bake at 375 degrees for 10–14 minutes or until golden brown.

Goes well with your favorite homemade stew or soup! How about your favorite Italian dish?

Daryle Singletary

Randy Travis and his wife, Lib Hatcher-Travis, brought Daryle Singletary to Music Town from Georgia. Travis and Travis were impressed with Singletary's traditional singing style and so was I!

"A country boy who sings country songs" best describes him. His biggest single is "I Let Her Lie," but my fave is "The Note."

Pretty soon after moving to Nashville, the likeable Singletary met Kerry, a singing girl from Texas, and they got married. The way they work holidays, according to Daryle, is that one year they visit the Singletary family at Thanksgiving and then visit his wife's folks in Texas at Christmas. The next year the couple visits his wife's relatives at Thanksgiving and Daryle's folks in Georgia at Christmas—"Keeping everybody happy," says Daryle.

These days, Daryle is managed by Erv Woolsey, who oversees the dynamite careers of George Strait, Lee Ann Womack, and Clay Walker. Daryle records for the Audium label.

The famous Wildhorse Saloon, Nashville, TN

Cornbread

4 cups cornmeal
2 teaspoons baking soda
2 teaspoons salt
4 eggs, beaten
4 cups buttermilk
⅓ cup bacon drippings

Preheat oven to 450 degrees. Combine dry ingredients and make a well in the center. Combine eggs and buttermilk and mix well. Add to cornmeal mixture and beat until smooth. Place bacon drippings in a 12" cast iron skillet. Heat in oven until hot and melted. Roll the drippings around the side of the pan; pour remaining into batter and stir. Pour batter into hot skillet. Bake for 35–45 minutes, or until a knife inserted in the center comes out clean and the top is golden brown.

Makes 6–8 servings.

"A country boy who sings country songs" best describes him.

Ricky & Sharon Skaggs

The first time I heard Ricky singing, he and Keith Whitley were with Ralph Stanley. It was so good it was scary.

As a child mandolin prodigy, Ricky traveled with mom Dorothy and dad Hobart as The Skaggs Family, playing churches and local theaters.

One night, as teenagers, he and picking pal Whitley went to see their hero, Ralph Stanley, and wound up onstage when Stanley's bus broke down. When he arrived, Stanley was impressed and soon hired them.

Skaggs later played in several other successful bluegrass bands, but his first taste of country music stardom was with the Emmylou Harris Hot Band. Among my favorite Skaggs tunes: "Uncle Pen" and "Highway 40 Blues."

In 1982, Skaggs accepted two CMA awards and fulfilled a lifetime dream when he joined the Grand Ole Opry. In 1985, he was named CMA Entertainer of the Year and picked up a Grammy. Skaggs also produced Dolly Parton's *White Limozeen* and has hosted both radio and TV shows.

Skaggs married Sharon White in 1981. They have two children, Molly and Lucas. Skaggs also has two children, Mandy and Andrew, from an earlier marriage.

Ricky & Sharon Skaggs

In Ricky & Sharon's home kitchen, 2001

The first time I heard Ricky, he and Keith Whitley were with Ralph Stanley. It was so good it was scary.

Grasshopper Pie

1 cup sugar
½ stick margarine, melted
3 eggs
1 teaspoon vanilla
½ teaspoon vinegar
½ cup chopped pecans
½ cup coconut
1 6-ounce bag chocolate chips
1 9" unbaked pie crust

Mix all ingredients and pour into an unbaked pie shell. Bake for 40–45 minutes at 350 degrees.

Connie Smith

Dolly Parton says, "There's only three female singers in the world: Streisand, Ronstadt, and Connie Smith. The rest of us are only pretending."

Connie came to Nashville at Bill Anderson's invitation. In 1965, she signed a deal with RCA when Chet Atkins heard her tape of Anderson's "Once A Day." Four months later, the song was number one. The following June she joined the Opry.

Stardom totally overwhelmed the shy singer who Roy Acuff called the "Sweetheart of the Grand Ole Opry." Connie hit big with "Once A Day" and "Ain't Had No Lovin'." In 1968, she felt so pressured, she contemplated ending it all—but found solace in Christianity. During the 1990's, Connie and Marty Stuart began co-writing. I ran into them once at the grocery store. "What are you two doing out on a rainy night like this?" I asked. The excuse they gave was so weak I ignored it. Marty says, "Hazel knew Connie and I were an item before *we* knew it." Lord knows that's not true.

They married. Princess meets handsome prince and lives happily ever after on the banks of the Cumberland River.

Seven-Layer Salad

When your favorite Opry members aren't on stage, many of them are in the kitchen. Each issue of the Circle Club newsletter brings a signature recipe from one of your Opry favorites.

Connie Smith says that a friend of hers from Ohio, Barb Sanders, gave her the recipe for seven-layer salad years ago. "I have always loved serving it to my family because inevitably there would be some ingredient in any food I served that one of my children wouldn't like—a common hazard with five children. With this salad, though, I was always able to hide things! Because the salad is all tossed and mixed together, my kids weren't able to notice any single ingredient as easily, and they would eat it without complaint." Connie still loves to serve the salad on holidays, and her kids ask for it every year.

Connie had a little fun recently after making the salad at a cooking show in Nashville. When asked by an audience member what her husband (and fellow Opry member) Marty Stuart's favorite dish was, Connie laughed, "I think I am!"

Dolly Parton says, "There's only three female singers in the world: Streisand, Ronstadt, and Connie Smith. The rest of us are only pretending."

1 head iceberg lettuce
3-5 ribs celery, diced
3-5 green onions, chopped
1 pound lean bacon
4 ounces (1 cup) shredded Cheddar cheese
4 ounces (1 cup) shredded Monterey Jack cheese
1 15-ounce can baby peas
1 8-ounce can water chestnuts
1 cup mayonnaise
1 cup ranch dressing
¼ cup milk
2 teaspoon Sweet 'N Low® or sugar

Wash and drain lettuce and tear into bite size pieces. Fry bacon until crisp; drain and crumble. Drain peas and water chestnuts. In a salad bowl, combine lettuce, celery, green onions, bacon, cheeses, peas, and water chestnuts. In a separate bowl, make the dressing by combining mayonnaise, ranch dressing, sugar, and milk; mix well. Add dressing to salad and toss. Cover and chill in refrigerator.

Makes 8 servings.

Statler Brothers

The first time I saw the Statler Brothers, they were opening for Johnny Cash, their timeless harmonies and stage antics leaving the audience totally ready for The Man in Black.

For my family, though, the Statlers' most important performance was a Saturday in June, 1967, at the Greensboro Coliseum. The death of my Caswell County, North Carolina, farming dad, William Boone, the Tuesday before, left Mama, Linnie Boone, my brothers Daniel and Henry Boone, and myself stunned. We had tickets for the Statlers' show and decided to attend. I never told the group this true story, but during the concert we laughed, we cried, we applauded, and, most importantly, we started to heal.

The Statlers first scored with "Flowers on the Wall" in 1965, then with hits like "Do You Know You Are My Sunshine" and "Elizabeth." Their TV show on The Nashville Network (TNN) drew the network's largest audience during the 1990's. Harold and Don Reid, Phil Balsley, and Jimmy Fortune are one of the most awarded groups in country music. They've sold over 15 million records, and to this day they sell out shows wherever they perform.

Mountain Pound Cake

½ pound (2 sticks) butter
½ cup shortening
1¾ cups sugar
5 eggs
3 cups flour
½ teaspoon baking powder
1 cup milk
3 teaspoon vanilla
½ teaspoon grated lemon peel (optional)

Cream butter, shortening, and sugar. Add eggs one at a time. Add flour and milk alternately; add baking powder with the last flour. Add vanilla. Mix for 5 minutes. Pour into a 10" greased and floured tube pan. Place in cold oven; then turn oven to 350 degrees and bake for 1 hour. Do not open oven even once! Let stand a few minutes before removing from pan.

...we cried, we laughed, we applauded, and, most importantly, we started to heal.

Boxley Style Chicken

8-10 chicken breasts, boned and skinless
2 2.25-ounce packages dried beef
1 pound bacon
1 10¾-ounce can cream of mushroom soup
1 8-ounce container sour cream

Preheat oven to 300 degrees. Cover bottom of large baking dish with dried beef. Wrap bacon around chicken breasts. Place wrapped chicken on top of dried beef. Mix soup and sour cream together until smooth and spread on top of chicken breasts. Place in oven and bake for 1½–2 hours.

Makes 8–10 servings.

George Strait

The Cowboy.

The first time I saw Strait sing live, I thought I'd died and gone to hillbilly heaven: I could not believe anybody could be that beautiful and sing that great.

I first met him at manager Erv Woolsey's office—we started a running joke about the scar under his chin. "Tell people Hazel bit you," I suggested, and he has ever since. This marvelous friendship has never wavered since that beginning. Never haughty, flirty, or vulgar, he is always a gentleman.

The secret of Strait's longevity: he is a real cowboy. The man cannot burn out on the hillbilly highway when he's roping cattle or horseback riding in Texas. His college-age son, Bubba, is his favorite roping partner; wife Norma has been his mainstay for 30 years.

George's signature song is "Love Without End, Amen," but I love "Does Fort Worth Ever Cross Your Mind." He recently told me that, above all, he loves to sing. "The recording will no doubt come to an end, but I will always sing. I love it," said the greatest cowboy of them all.

George Strait

King Ranch Chicken

1 10¾-ounce can cream of chicken soup
1 10¾-ounce can cream of mushroom soup
¾ cup chicken broth
½ 10-ounce can Ro*Tel® tomatoes with green chili peppers
4 chicken breast halves, boned and skinless
1 6-ounce package corn tortillas, cut into 6 pieces
1 medium onion, chopped
½ pound shredded Cheddar cheese

Preheat oven to 350 degrees. Mix together the first 4 ingredients and set aside. In a greased 9"x13" casserole, layer the ingredients in the following order: chicken, tortillas, onions, and soup mixture. Top with cheese. Bake for 1 hour or until mixture is bubbly.

The first time I saw Strait sing live, I thought I'd died and gone to hillbilly heaven: I could not believe anybody could be that beautiful and sing that great.

Spanish Rice

1 cup raw rice
2 tablespoons vegetable shortening
1 small onion, chopped
½ green bell pepper, chopped
1½ teaspoons salt
2 teaspoon chili powder
1 10-ounce can tomatoes, chopped
2 cups water

In a skillet, brown rice in shortening over medium heat for about 10 minutes. Add onion and bell pepper. Stir. Add salt, chili powder, and tomatoes, including juice. Add water. Cover and simmer 30–35 minutes, or until rice is tender and liquid is absorbed.

Me and George at the premier of his movie, Pure Country

Marty Stuart

Marty Stuart was on the road playing bluegrass with The Sullivans when he was 10 years old. Soon, he was playing and singing with Lester Flatt & the Nashville Grass—at the tender age of 12.

In 1989, a grown-up Marty launched a string of successes; and in 1993 joined the Grand Ole Opry. I love his "Hillbilly Rock." His duet with Travis Tritt, "The Whiskey Ain't Workin' Anymore," led to a Duo of the Year Award. And *The Pilgrim*, his last album for MCA, should have gone double-platinum.

After closing the MCA door, God opened two windows for Marty. The first was marrying Connie Smith, whom Marty had loved since he was 12 years old. Second, Marty had a role in Steven Seagal's *Fire Down Below*, and became acquainted with Billy Bob Thornton. I was proud when Marty got a 2001 Golden Globe nomination for his *All The Pretty Horses* soundtrack. And I was not surprised when Billy Bob had Marty produce his *Private Radio* CD on Lost Highway Records.

Singer, songwriter, musician extraordinaire, photographer, movie soundtrack-meister, Marty is happy being busy and busy being happy.

Marty Stuart

Fudge Pie

Marty's mother Hilda's recipe

- **1 cup sugar**
- **3 tablespoons all-purpose flour**
- **3 tablespoons cocoa**
- **1 teaspoon vanilla**
- **2 eggs**
- **½ cup milk**
- **3 tablespoons melted margarine**

Mix dry ingredients; add beaten eggs, milk, vanilla, and margarine. Pour into a greased 9" pie plate. Bake 30–35 minutes at 350 degrees. Allow to cool for 20 minutes, then chill for 2 hours. Serve with whipped cream if desired.

Makes 8 servings.

I was proud when Marty got a 2001 Golden Globe nomination for his <u>All the Pretty Horses</u> soundtrack.

Me and Marty at his book signing, 2000

Chalee Tennison

Like Willie Nelson, Chalee Tennison is from Texas. Like Tammy Wynette when she arrived in Nashville in 1965, she is the single mother of three children.

With her music, Chalee shares the emotions of a mother/woman in songs like "Go Back" and "Someone Else's Turn To Cry." Music has been healing for the singer and she wants others to be touched by what she feels.

The 33-year old former prison guard was no flitty teeny-bopper when she released her self-titled Asylum CD in 1999, and no pop wannabe when her second album, *This Woman's Heart*, debuted. Chalee is a stone-country singer, and she isn't ashamed to keep the tear in a sad song.

Chalee comes from a large family who likes to sing. She says when her grandmother died in Clute, Texas, she had 172 grandchildren. When Chalee was a kid, her grandmother used to sit her and her sisters on the hearth and tell them to sing with their mom. "Just a family of singers," she remembers.

With three kids of her own, you can believe Chalee knows how to cook.

Chalee Tennison

Chicken Spaghetti

1 hen
2 7-ounce packages of spaghetti
2 medium (8-ounce) cans tomato sauce
3 large onions
1 cup celery, diced
½ pound grated cheese
1 green bell pepper, diced
2 tablespoon chili powder
1 can cream of mushroom soup

Boil hen until tender. Remove meat from bone and cut up. Skim fat from broth and reserve. Cook spaghetti in 2 quarts broth for 5 minutes. Brown onions, green pepper, and celery in 3 tablespoons of reserved fat. Add spaghetti and chicken, mushroom soup, and tomato sauce. Cook on low very slowly for 1 hour. Mix in part of the cheese and pour into a 9"x13" casserole dish. Sprinkle the rest of cheese on top and bake a few minutes until cheese melts.

Makes 20 servings.

Chalee is a stone-country singer, and she isn't ashamed to keep the tear in a sad song.

Hot Cabbage Slaw

4 cups shredded red or green cabbage
1 16-ounce can cut green beans, drained
¼ cup sugar
1 tablespoon instant minced onion
1 teaspoon salt
½ cup vinegar

In a large saucepan, heat cabbage, green beans, sugar, onion, salt, and vinegar to boiling. Reduce heat and simmer uncovered, tossing occasionally, until cabbage is crisp-tender, about 5–7 minutes.

Makes 6–8 servings.

Pam Tillis

But success has not changed beautiful Pam one iota.

Gold and platinum albums line her hallway. She's world famous for tunes like "Queen of Denial" and "Mi Vida Loca (My Crazy Life)." But success has not changed beautiful Pam one iota.

Her daddy, Mel Tillis, is one of the most respected men in country music. He accepted the Entertainer of the Year trophy in 1976. Ironically, Pam's first hit was penned by dad's pal Harlan Howard, who also wrote Mel's first hit in 1967.

Pam has written many of her own hits and has had her songs recorded by others. She was the first female country star to perform on Broadway in *Smokey Joe's Café*. But Pam says her proudest moments were when she gave birth to her son, Ben, and her Grand Ole Opry induction in 2000.

I shall never forget watching as Mel's eldest, dressed in red, became a bona fide member of the Opry. She's done the Tillis name proud, and I proudly call this fine lady my friend.

Pam Tillis

Stewed Apples

Best served as a side dish.

4-5 Granny Smith apples, peeled and sliced
¼ cup orange juice
½ cup brown sugar
2 tablespoons butter
1 teaspoon vanilla

Put apple slices in a medium saucepan with orange juice, brown sugar, butter, and vanilla. Cook over medium heat until tender, about 10–20 minutes.

I use vanilla I make myself from 4–5 vanilla beans I buy at the health food store. Split the beans length-wise with a sharp knife and put into a bottle of vodka for 3–4 weeks. You will have a great tasting vanilla for all your cooking. It's wonderful and makes great Christmas gifts when put in corked bottles. I pour hot wax over corks to seal the bottles well.

Having fun at the recording studio in Nashville, 2001

Salmon Croquettes

1 pound salmon
1 egg
1 small onion, chopped
¼ cup yellow corn meal
1 teaspoon curry powder
canola oil

Mix together salmon, egg, onion, corn meal, and curry powder. Make into small patties and fry in an iron skillet in a small amount of canola oil. Cook on both sides until lightly browned (about 8–10 minutes) or until done.

Makes 6 servings.

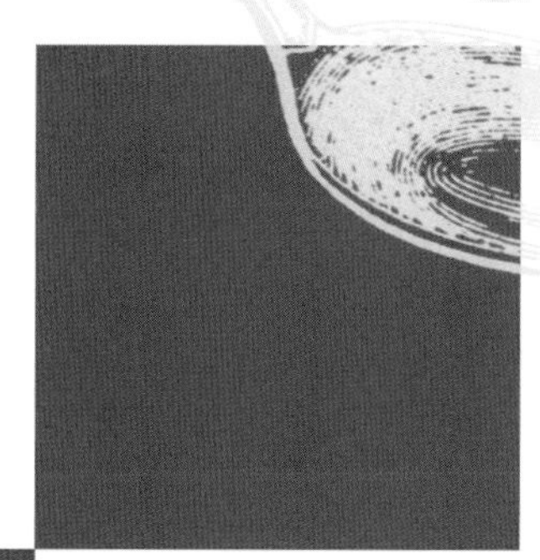

I shall never forget watching as Mel's eldest, dressed in red, became a bona fide member of the Opry.

Aaron Tippin

My dear friend Robert K. Oermann turned me on to Aaron Tippin before he got a record deal. "You gotta hear this guy," said the journalist. The corporate airplane pilot turned songwriter and hillbilly singer sang so much like Hank Williams I felt a tear trickle from my eye, straight from the heart. I'd up the volume every time "You've Got to Stand For Something" came on the radio, and I loved "There Ain't Nothin' Wrong With The Radio."

Aaron married a songwriter, Thea. Their first son, Teddy, was born in 1997, and a second son, Thomas, arrived three years later. Aaron's 22-year-old daughter Charla also lives with them at their fabulous country digs near Smithville, Tennessee.

Doug Howard at Lyric Street Records told me I would dig the Tip's new album and I did. My favorite song was "Kiss This"—an answer to Faith Hill's "This Kiss." His tune topped the charts for three weeks and the Tip sold enough *People Like Us* albums to hit the charts at number five. There's an old country saying: "Good guys finish first." Aaron Tippin is living proof that that's true.

Aaron Tippin

There's an old country saying, "Good guys finish first." Aaron Tippin is living proof that that's true.

Mom's Ambrosia

8-10 small naval oranges
1 8-ounce can crushed pineapple, or pineapple tidbits
1 6-ounce jar maraschino cherries, drained
½ cup chopped pecans
½ cup shredded coconut

Peel and cut oranges into sections and put in a large bowl. Add pineapple. Cut cherries in half and add to mixture. Stir in pecans and coconut. Refrigerate for 1 hour.

Makes 6–8 servings.

Chicken Goulash

1 14.5-ounce can mixed vegetables
2 6-ounce cans chicken
1 4.5-ounce package of Lipton® chicken-flavored rice
salt and pepper to taste

In pot, prepare chicken-flavored rice by package directions. When cooked, add drained can of mixed vegetables and drained cans of chicken. Stir together over low heat and add salt and pepper to taste.

This meal is fast, cheap, and easy.

Meatballs and Sauce

1½ pounds lean ground beef
onion salt or minced onions to taste
1 tablespoon oregano
1 tablespoon basil
salt and pepper
2 14.5-ounce cans whole tomatoes

In a medium bowl, combine beef, onion salt, oregano, basil, salt and pepper. Mix well. Form into small meatballs, about 1½". In a saucepan, brown meatballs over medium high heat. Pour off excess fat and add tomatoes. Cover and let simmer on low heat for 1 hour. Serve over pasta.

Makes 6–8 servings.

Shania Twain's life story will one day be a movie. Raised in Ontario, Canada, 21-year-old Shania was left to raise three younger siblings when her parents died. She kept the family together by singing.

Her debut album set the singer up for superstardom. Producer Mutt Lange saw her video on CMT, watched Shania perform at Fan Fair, and got her phone number. By the time the couple wed the following December, they'd written half an album, mostly by phone.

Shania is so pretty, she makes you think of Barbie™. She's a little stand-offish until she gets to know you, and then she's really sweet. At the BMI Awards 2000, Shania spied me across a room of a thousand people, made a beeline, and, with tears in her eyes, hugged me. We talked about Switzerland, where she and Mutt raise roses. Shania said, "I really cook. I want to be in your cookbook."

Shania's hits include "Any Man of Mine" and "You're Still The One." Her third album, *Come On Over*, has sold more than any other recording by a female. Thank you, Shania, for the recipe from Switzerland.

Potato Roast

4 potatoes (peeled or unpeeled)
3-4 garlic cloves, sliced into slivers
1 tablespoon dry parsley flakes
1 bay leaf
½ teaspoon salt
sprinkle of pepper
4 tablespoon olive oil

Optional (for variety):

4 tablespoon white cooking wine
1 teaspoon rosemary

Chop potatoes in quarters. Combine all ingredients in a roasting pot. Toss until potatoes are covered evenly. Place lid on pot and roast at 200–250 degrees for 4–5 hours for a slow roast or at 450 degrees for 45 minutes for a quick roast. Keep an eye on it in case your oven is really hot; it may cook even faster. Stir 15–20 minutes into baking.

Makes 4–6 servings.

Shania spied me across a room with a thousand people, made a beeline, and, with tears in her eyes, hugged me.

About the hottest act on the country scene today is Down Under's keith urban. Why lower case? "It's hip," says Aussie urban. "The Internet is all lower case, so I thought it would be cool and get attention."

Being cool and getting attention is his energized on-stage performance. urban was everywhere the week of the Country Radio Seminar. He made three appearances, each time earning a standing 'O.' He sang his hit "Your Everything," and his number-one, "But For the Grace of God," which brought screams. But nobody had ever seen anything like his unbelievably hot picking as he danced all over the stage and into the audience, smiling and dancing. I can't describe it!

The hunky urban could go rock, but he was raised on country music. His parents, fans of Dolly Parton, Charley Pride, and Don Williams, had all their records, so urban learned their songs and began singing at a very young age. He had four number-one songs in his native Australia before migrating to Music City, the place he now calls home. Thanks to keith's mom for sending this special recipe all the way from Australia.

keith urban

Impossible Quiche

- ¾ cup plain flour
- 4 eggs
- 2½ tablespoons soft butter
- 2 cups milk
- 1 large onion, diced
- ½ cup unprocessed bran
- 1 teaspoon each basil, salt, and pepper
- 3 slices bacon, diced
- ½ cup grated mild Cheddar or Swiss cheese

Mix first 4 ingredients with electric mixer; add other ingredients. Pour into greased pan. Bake for 1 hour at 325 degrees.

I also put in either sliced zucchini or a mixture of vegetables.

Cooking up fun at the studio, 2001

The hunky urban could go rock, but he was raised on country music.

Phil Vassar

Generally, award-winning songwriters do not make successful recording artists. But Phil Vassar is an exception. His debut Arista single, "Carlene," climbed to number four, and his follow up single, "Just Another Day In Paradise," went number one. The singer/songwriter wrote all 11 songs on his self-titled CD, co-produced with Byron Gallimore.

It came as no surprise when Vassar was named Songwriter of the Year by ASCAP in 1999. His list of hits includes "Right On The Money" (Alan Jackson), "I'm Alright" and "Bye Bye" (Jo Dee Messina), "Little Red Rodeo" (Collin Raye), and "For A Little While" and "My Next Thirty Years" (Tim McGraw).

During 2000, the singer opened shows for the hugely successful Tim McGraw/Faith Hill *Soul 2 Soul* Tour and joined Kenny Rogers for several dates. He also opened a bevy of sold-out shows for Kenny Chesney, who calls Vassar the most talented person he's ever met. Singer/songwriter/musician Vassar also co-produced tracks for Marshall Dyllon's debut CD and wrote the group's "Live It Up."

Pumpkin Bread

Phil Vassar

When Phil was a little fella, holiday cooking was something he always wanted to be a part of, especially when it came to stirring the batch of pumpkin bread, then eating the first loaf out of the oven!
—Dianne, Phil's Mom

- **3½ cups flour**
- **1½ teaspoons salt**
- **2 teaspoons soda**
- **1 teaspoon cinnamon**
- **1 teaspoon nutmeg**
- **3 cups sugar**
- **1 cup oil**
- **⅔ cup water**
- **4 eggs, beaten**
- **1 15-ounce can pumpkin**
- **1 cup chopped nuts (optional)**

Sift flour, salt, soda, spices, and sugar together in a large bowl. Add oil, water, eggs, and pumpkin and beat until smooth. Stir in nuts; pour batter into three 4"x8" greased loaf pans. Bake in preheated 350-degree oven for 1 hour. Cool in pans on cooling racks for 10 minutes.

Makes 3 loaves.

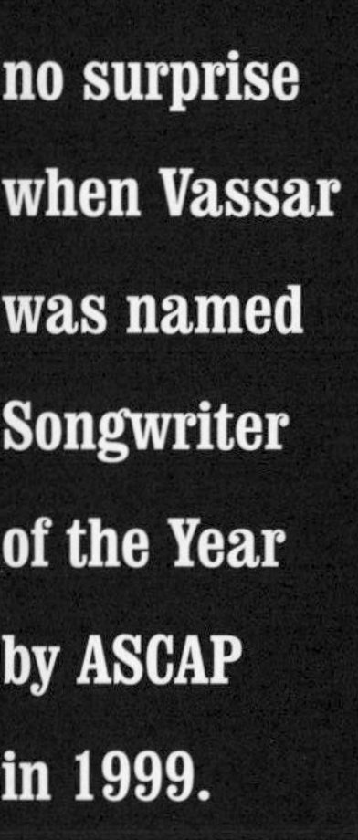

It came as no surprise when Vassar was named Songwriter of the Year by ASCAP in 1999.

Recipe for a Happy Day!

This was in a cookbook we compiled when the kids were in school—I thought it was pretty good "food for thought!"
—Dianne, Phil's mom

- **1 cup of friendly words**
- **4 heaping tablespoons of time and patience**
- **2 heaping cups of understanding**
- **pinch of warm personality**
- **dash of humor**

Measure words carefully. Add heaping cups of understanding. Use generous amounts of time and patience. Cook on front burner, keeping temperature low. Do not boil! Add a dash of humor and a pinch of warm personality. Season to taste with the spice of life… serve in individual molds.

Clay Walker

I cannot believe Clay Walker has just released his seventh album. The Beaumont, Texas, native has scored 11 number-one records, including the almost spiritual "The Chain of Love" and "This Woman And This Man."

Walker has racked up four platinum albums and two gold albums since he came on the country music scene in 1993. His most recent album contains "La Bamba," which he sings in perfect Spanish. Walker worked for years mastering the language so that when a Latino heard him sing they wouldn't say, "That's a gringo."

For his fifth appearance at the mammoth Rodeo Houston, the singer made a dramatic entrance into the arena riding a tall chestnut horse. Those country music/rodeo-loving Texans gave Walker a high-decibel squawl.

Although he has been diagnosed with multiple sclerosis, he has not slowed down. He continues to perform a full concert schedule and works around his beautiful Texas spread. His wife, Lori, and children, McClay and Skylor, are the light of Clay's life.

Those country music/rodeo-loving Texans gave Walker a high-decibel squawl.

Clay Walker

Carrot Cake

- 2 cups sugar
- 1 cup oil
- 4 eggs
- 2 cups flour
- 2 teaspoons baking powder
- 1½ teaspoons baking soda
- 1 teaspoon salt
- 2 teaspoons cinnamon
- 3 cups grated carrot
- ½ cup chopped pecans

Cream sugar and oil. Add eggs and beat well. Sift together dry ingredients and add to sugar mixture. Fold in carrots and pecans. Pour into 2 greased and floured 9" pans. Bake at 350 degrees for 35 minutes.

Makes 2 layers.

Cream Cheese Icing

- 1 stick margarine
- 8 ounces cream cheese
- 1 teaspoon vanilla
- 1 pound powdered sugar
- 1 cup finely chopped pecans

Cream together margarine and cream cheese. Add vanilla. Beat in powdered sugar. Fold in pecans. Spread generously between layers, then on sides and top.

Nutritional Value: "What's it to you!"

Dottie West heard Steve Wariner play bass when he was just 17 and hired him on the spot.

Steve loves to tell of his first Grand Ole Opry appearance. The Opry host was announcing Dottie's name as the always-late performer wheeled her Cadillac into the alley between the Ryman Auditorium and Tootsie's. Scared to death, Steve grabbed his bass and followed Dottie up the steps past Ernest Tubb, Marty Robbins, and Roy Acuff. "I made it through, but I don't know how," he laughs.

Wariner began writing songs at 16 and recording his songs at 24 on RCA Records with his mentor, Chet Atkins. My favorite Wariner song from this era was "Midnight Fire"—I still request that song on WSM. He capped off a long string of hits with "Holes In The Floor of Heaven," the CMA Song and Single of the Year in 1998.

Singer, songwriter, musician, record producer, magician, and all-round nice guy, there just isn't a better person than Steve Wariner. He, wife Caryn, and sons Ryan and Ross reside in a lovely home in Franklin, Tennessee, where—lucky me—this picture of Steve and me was taken.

Steve Wariner

With the perfect hosts–at home with the Wariners, 2001

Apple Pie

pastry for two-crust pie
6 cups thinly sliced, peeled apples
1 tablespoon lemon juice
2 tablespoons flour
¾ teaspoon cinnamon
¼ teaspoon salt
⅛ teaspoon nutmeg
½ cup sugar

Preheat oven to 425 degrees. Line a 9" pie pan with 1 pastry crust. In a large bowl, toss apples with lemon juice. Add flour, cinnamon, salt, nutmeg, and sugar. Gently mix. Spoon apples in prepared pie crust; top with remaining pastry. Press together to seal and flute the edges. Cut slits in top of pastry. I like to decorate the top with cut-out leaves made of pastry. Bake for 45 minutes or until apples are tender and crust is brown. Be sure to put pie on a baking sheet before cooking so you won't dirty your oven.

Singer, songwriter, musician, record producer, magician, and all-round nice guy, there just isn't a better person than Steve.

Corn Soufflé

Caryn Wariner

2 tablespoons unsalted butter
2 tablespoons flour
1 cup milk
3 medium eggs, separated
2 cups fresh corn kernels
2 teaspoons sugar
1 teaspoon salt
¼ teaspoon white pepper

Preheat oven to 350 degrees. Grease a 6-cup soufflé dish. Melt butter in a medium saucepan over medium heat and sprinkle with flour. Cook until well blended, about 3 minutes. Whisk in milk and cook until thick, about 5 minutes. Beat yolks with a fork. Pour yolk into sauce and whisk. Cook another minute. Off the heat, whisk the rest of the ingredients, except egg whites, into mixture and let cool 3 minutes. Whisk egg whites into soft peaks and fold into corn mixture. Pour into soufflé dish and bake 30–35 minutes.

Makes 6 servings.

Warren Brothers

Songwriter Harlan Howard says of the Warren Brothers, "What I love about these guys, besides they remind me of Willie and Waylon when they were young, is they represent what country music used to be and needs to be again. Namely, people singing, dancing, drinking, and good-looking girls everywhere."

Brad and younger brother Brett have been in bands together since they were kids. For years they'd play three shows daily, 300 days a year in Tampa beach bars, bail out for Nashville, go broke, and go back to the bars. With hit albums like *King of Nothing* and singles like "Move On," the Warrens will never return to the bars of Tampa again.

The brothers have toured with Tim McGraw, Faith Hill, and The Dixie Chicks, and appeared at George Strait's Country Festival 2001. This crazed twosome knows how to have fun. At RCA chief Joe Galante's big 5-0 surprise birthday party, Brad gave me quite a kiss and swore I kissed him back. I didn't. See, at my stage in life, I was so shocked by getting kissed like that, I couldn't remember what I was supposed to do!

This crazed twosome knows how to have fun.

Second Avenue, Nashville, T

Warren Brothers

Brad and younger brother Brett have been in bands together since they were kids.

The Warren Brothers Dip

- **1 cup mayonnaise**
- **1 medium red onion, thinly sliced**
- **1 pound Jarlsberg cheese, cut in cubes**
- **½ teaspoon garlic powder**
- **½ teaspoon black pepper**

Mix all in a medium bowl. Pour into a glass pie dish and bake at 350 degrees for 30 minutes or until hot and bubbly. Serve with crackers.

The Whites

Could they sing! When Emmylou Harris heard them she remarked, "They sound like angels."

When I moved to Nashville in 1970, my first friends were The Whites.

Back then they were the Down Home Folks, Buck and his five girls—wife Pat and daughters Sharon, Cheryl, Rosie, and Melissa. I remember those girls laughing and smiling all the time, a trait they inherited honestly from their mother.

Could they sing! When Emmylou Harris heard them she remarked, "They sound like angels." All the young musicians/singers fell in love with those beautiful White girls, but Buck guarded his daughters with his life. His mandolin looked as deadly to suitors as a gun. But Pat always had back-home Texas pinto beans steaming in a pot to oblige a hungry musician's belly.

Pat traveled the road with Buck, Sharon, and Cheryl until Rosie and Melissa cried for their mama and she chose to stay home. When Buck, Cheryl, and Sharon got a major record deal, they were renamed The Whites.

I loved The Whites' top-10 hits, "Hangin' Around" and "It Sure Rains Hard in Tennessee." The Opry's First Family, they are some of country music's most respected entertainers.

Chocolate Cake

The Whites' recipe

- 2½ cups sugar
- 1 cup Crisco®
- 2 eggs
- 1 cup buttermilk
- 2 teaspoon baking soda
- 2½ cups all-purpose flour
- ¼ cup cocoa
- ½ teaspoon salt
- 1 teaspoon vanilla
- 1 cup boiling water

In a large bowl, mix sugar, Crisco®, and eggs. Stir soda in buttermilk. Add to sugar/Crisco®/egg mixture and mix well. Add flour, cocoa, and salt. Stir in vanilla and boiling water. Pour into a greased and floured 9"x13" pan and bake in a preheated oven at 350 degrees for 40 minutes. Frost while hot.

Frosting

- 2 tablespoon cocoa
- 2 cups sugar
- ½ cup milk
- ½ cup butter
- ¼ teaspoon salt
- 1 teaspoon vanilla

Mix all ingredients except vanilla in a saucepan and bring to a boil, stirring well. Cook until a drop of mixture forms a soft ball in cold water. Then boil 2 minutes longer. Add vanilla and beat until mixture is cool enough to spread on warm cake. Delicious.

The Whites are the Grand Ole Opry's first family. Texans by birth, Buck's Aunt Kathryn would bake this cake for her 5 sons and taught Pat to make it.

The Opry's First Family, they are some of country music's most respected entertainers.

Turkey Dressing

Pat White's recipe

- 2 tablespoons vegetable shortening
- 2 cups self-rising cornmeal
- 1¾ cups buttermilk
- ½ loaf (10 slices) white bread
- 2 large onions, chopped
- 2 ribs celery, chopped
- 1 stick (½ cup) butter
- 5 eggs
- 3 tablespoons dried sage (or 2 tablespoons powdered)
- 1 tablespoon cider vinegar
- 1 teaspoon salt
- 1 teaspoon pepper
- turkey broth

Preheat oven to 450 degrees. In a 10" iron skillet, heat shortening until almost smoking; combine cornmeal and buttermilk. Mix well and pour into small skillet. Bake for 20 minutes or until golden brown. Cool and crumble into a large bowl. Toast white bread slices, cut into squares, and mix with cornbread. In a skillet, sauté onions and celery in butter until tender. Add to cornbread mixture. Boil 3 of the eggs until hard cooked; cool and chop. Add boiled eggs and remaining 3 eggs to cornbread mixture. Add sage, vinegar, salt, and pepper. Mix well. Add turkey broth to make a mixture the consistency of cake batter. Pour into a greased and floured pan. Bake at 350 degrees for 45 minutes.

Makes 10–12 servings.

The Wilkinsons

When this father-daughter-son trio moved to Tennessee from Canada in 1997, they had no idea record labels would vie for their sweet harmony and a song titled "26¢." In one year, The Wilkinsons were the biggest new act in country music.

The family's pure love of singing is evident throughout their debut CD, *Nothing But Love,* their second album, *Here And Now,* and songs like "Jimmy's Got a Girlfriend." Amanda and Tyler have matured vocally, and as people. Tyler is a handsome young hunk with girls going gaga over his good looks and great singing. Amanda has matured into a woman with movie-star appeal who sings better all the time. Steve is the songwriter for the group, writing six of the songs on their new album.

I've observed this family often—backstage at the Opry, at the ASCAP Banquet 2000, shopping, eating in restaurants, and on Music Row. They always have ready smiles, good manners, a kind word, and a handshake. As Giant Records' exec and producer Doug Johnson says, "The world needs to know The Wilkinsons. They make it a better place." Amen, Brother Johnson. Amen.

The Wilkinsons

Banana Cake with Royal York Dressing

- 2⅓ cups all-purpose flour
- 1¼ teaspoons baking powder
- 1 teaspoon baking soda
- 1⅔ cups sugar
- 1 teaspoon salt
- ⅔ cup shortening
- ⅔ cup fully ripe bananas, mashed
- place 2 teaspoons lemon juice in a measuring cup and add milk to make ⅔ cup (sour milk)
- 2 eggs
- ⅔ cup chopped walnuts

Sift together flour, baking powder, baking soda, sugar, and salt in a large bowl. Add the shortening, bananas, and sour milk. Mix until flour is dampened. Beat vigorously for 2 minutes. Add eggs and beat 2 minutes longer. Stir in walnuts. Bake in 2 greased and floured 9"x1⅛" rounded pans in 360 degree oven for 30–35 minutes. Cool 10 minutes in pans. Remove and cool.

Royal York Dressing:

- 1 cup milk
- 3 tablespoons flour
- ½ cup butter
- ½ cup Crisco® or lard
- 1 cup powdered sugar
- 1 tablespoon vanilla

Mix flour and milk and bring to a boil over low heat while stirring. Let cool for 5 minutes, stirring occasionally. Cream butter and Crisco® and add sugar and vanilla. Then add flour mixture all at once and beat 2–3 minutes.

Spread the Royal York Dressing over the Banana Cake and let sit for 5 minutes.

...and they always have ready smiles, good manners, a kind word, and a handshake.

Lee Ann Womack

The slogan of the Nashville Songwriters Association International (NSAI) is, "It All Begins With a Song." Never was that truer than with "I Hope You Dance," which catapulted Lee Ann Womack to superstardom.

The first time I heard it I had to pull off the road. The next day, the video floored me. "That song is going to be a giant step for that little gal from Jacksonville, Texas," I reported on radio. "It's a career song, her signature song, a major hit." My prediction was more than accurate. After the tune spent six weeks at number one, Womack was invited to the Nobel Prize Concert in Oslo, Norway, in December 2000.

Womack, whose hits include "The Fool," was invited by special invitation from President and Mrs. George W. Bush to perform for their first formal White House dinner. Lee Ann, who home-schools daughter Aubrie, reportedly talked with the First Lady about education in this country. Awarded Single of the Year and Song of the Year by the CMA, the album *I Hope You Dance* is reaching double-platinum status while the singer reaches for the stars.

Lee Ann Womack

Brownies

- **1 cup butter**
- **½ cup cocoa**
- **4 eggs**
- **2 cups sugar**
- **1½ cups all-purpose flour**
- **dash of salt**
- **1 teaspoon vanilla**
- **1 cup chocolate morsels (optional)**
- **1 cup chopped pecans (optional)**

Preheat oven to 350 degrees. Melt butter; dissolve cocoa in butter and set aside. Beat eggs and sugar together until light and fluffy. Beat in flour, salt, and vanilla. Add cocoa and butter to flour mixture. At this point, add optional ingredients. Bake in a greased and floured 9"x13" metal pan for 30–40 minutes. Bake for 30 minutes for chewy brownies or 40 minutes for cake-like brownies.

Sometimes I add a little extra cocoa. But be sure to add a little extra sugar if you do.

...the album I Hope You Dance is reaching toward double platinum status while the singer reaches for the stars.

Cool and in control, Chely wept with joy.

Chely Wright

Chely Wright is one of the prettiest girls in country music and one of the hardest workers. When she isn't performing, she's writing or co-writing with pals like Brad Paisley, with whom she penned "Hard To Be A Husband, Hard To Be A Wife."

After several seasons at Opryland and a couple of other record deals, Chely convinced MCA's Tony Brown she belonged on his label—with him producing. "Single White Female" kicked her first album of the same title to gold. Chely arrived at MCA for what she thought was a meeting, and the entire staff screamed *Surprise!* when she walked in the door. Cool and in control, Chely wept with joy. We're talking about a girl who, at 3 years old, when asked what she wanted to be, broke into "Hey Loretta."

Her Reading, Writing and Rhythm Foundation provides musical instruments and equipment to schools. It's a right thing in a sometimes wrong world to help the Wright foundation—just write a check.

Chely Wright

Baked Corn

2 cups corn
2 tablespoons margarine
1 teaspoon salt
2 tablespoons flour
1 cup milk
2 tablespoons sugar
2 eggs, beaten

Grease a 1 quart casserole dish. Combine ingredients and pour into casserole dish. Bake in a 300 degree oven for about 1 hour and 20 minutes.

Chely Wright is one of the prettiest girls in country music and one of the hardest workers.

Ham and Potato Cheesy Bake

2 large potatoes, uncooked
1 cup chopped green bell pepper
1 cup cubed Velveeta® cheese
1 cup ham, cubed
salt and pepper to taste

Grease a 1 quart glass casserole dish. Cut potatoes into ½" cubes. Mix potatoes, green pepper, cheese, and ham. Add salt and pepper to taste. Microwave on high 18–20 minutes, stirring occasionally.

Makes 4–6 servings.

Trisha Yearwood

God has blessed Trisha Yearwood with a voice like a finely tuned Stradivarius. She can sing "She's In Love With the Boy" and "XXX'S & OOO'S (An American Girl)" or duet with Pavarotti—the gamut!

"Best female demo singer on Music Row is Trisha Yearwood," you used to overhear at watering holes and meat-plus-threes in the early days of her career. When she and her husband separated, Trisha moved into a condo where I had an office. I recall sharing the elevator with her and her dirty laundry. Even sans makeup, her natural, innocent beauty was breathtaking.

The Monticello, Georgia, native was tearfully happy when she was named the CMA's Female Vocalist of the Year in 1997 and 1998. I was honored to be at the Ryman when Trisha was stunned by Ricky Skaggs' invitation to join the Opry and equally honored to be onstage when she was officially made an Opry member.

Other Opry members told me that the love they feel for Trisha—which I quoted on my morning radio program—was genuine. Watching her backstage, it's obvious Trisha loves them back.

Three Bread Dressing

"This is my Grandma Lizzie's cornbread dressing recipe that my mom now makes every Thanksgiving. Sometimes I will make this recipe in the summer, just because I am lonesome for home and family!" —Trisha Yearwood

- 1 pound cornbread (your own favorite recipe or the Buttermilk Cornbread recipe)
- ½ pound toasted bread crumbs (make your own from ½ loaf of white bread cut into ½ inch cubes and toasted slow in oven until lightly browned)
- ¼ pound saltine crackers
- ½ medium onion, finely chopped
- 3 eggs, boiled and chopped
- 1-1½ quart broth saved from baking turkey or hen (skim fat)
- salt and pepper to taste

Sauté onions in 2 tablespoons of fat until clear. Don't brown. In a very large container (gallon or larger), crumble breads and crackers, add onions and eggs. Toss and add broth until mixture is well-moistened. Clean hands make great mixers! Add salt and pepper to taste. Place in a 9"x13" baking pan that has been sprayed with non-stick cooking spray. Bake 15 minutes at 450 degrees until lightly browned.

Together before her big Opry performance, 2001

She can sing "She's in Love with the Boy" and "XXX's and OOO's (An American Girl)" or duet with Pavarotti—the gamut!

Buttermilk Cornbread

- 3 cups self-rising buttermilk cornbread mix
- 2 tablespoons melted butter or bacon drippings
- 2-3 cups buttermilk (enough to make a thick batter)

Mix all ingredients. Pour into well-greased 10" iron skillet. Bake at 450 degrees until well browned, about 20 minutes. The browned crust adds flavor to the dressing!

Wildhorse Saloon

In 1994, the Wildhorse Saloon opened its doors right in tune with the line-dancing craze popularized by "Achy Breaky Heart," the song that made Billy Ray Cyrus a household name. Line dancing on TNN went together like meringue on lemon pie, and it was live from Nashville's historic Second Avenue venue, The Wildhorse Saloon.

Stars like the Judds and Kathy Mattea utilized the facility for Fan Fair parties. Record labels used it as a venue to showcase new acts and new acts showcased for record labels. Lonestar signed a proxy record deal on a Wildhorse napkin after performing for label head Joe Galante. Fans in long lines curving south toward Broadway went for entertainment and food. Yep, the Wildhorse has quite a reputation for its vittles—especially fried dill pickles.

Everybody wants to go to the Wildhorse Saloon in Nashville. Why just this year, Russell Crowe, best actor at the 2001 Academy Awards®, was on-stage at the Wildhorse with his friend, newcomer Jamie O'Neal.

Streusel Cornbread

Wildhorse Saloon

Chris Rains, Executive Chef

At the Wildhorse Saloon, this recipe is made in large quantities. The recipe below has been adapted for home use.

Cornbread

- **2½ cups buttermilk self-rising cornmeal mix**
- **2 whole eggs**
- **1 cup milk or water**
- **¼ cup granulated sugar**
- **½ cup cut corn kernels**
- **½ cup shredded Cheddar cheese**
- **1½ tablespoons dark corn syrup**

Streusel Topping

- **½ cup butter (1 stick), softened**
- **½ cup brown sugar**
- **1 tablespoons honey**
- **1⅔ cups flour**

Preheat oven to 350 degrees. Grease a 9"x9" pan. Combine cornmeal mix, eggs, milk, sugar, corn, cheese, and syrup. Mix well and pour into prepared pan. Bake for 15 minutes. Prepare streusel topping with an electric mixer; whip the butter, brown sugar, and honey for 1 minute. Add flour a little at a time until blended. After baking for 15 minutes, add crumbled streusel topping and bake additional 10–15 minutes.

Makes 9 squares.

Recipe Index

Appetizer

Salad

Soup

Entree

Recipe Index

Side Dish

Bread

Dessert

Credits

Photo Credits

We greatly appreciate all of the Nashville record labels, publicity managers, and friends who arranged for the use of the artists' publicity photographs.

Rutherford Studios is responsible for all the food and Nashville scene photography on pages 6–116. Rutherford Studios is also responsible for the photography of the following artists: Bill Anderson, Renee Bell, Brooks & Dunn, Tony Brown, Pete Fisher, Fletcher Foster, Joe & Phran Galante, Vince Gill, Andy Griggs, Oak Ridge Boys, SHeDAISY, Ricky Skaggs, Hazel Smith, Pam Tillis, keith urban, Steve Wariner, and Trisha Yearwood.

Jeff Frazier is responsible for the Robert Earl Keen photography.

The Aaron Tippin photos are used by permission of Lyric Street Records.

A special thank you to international photographer Michele Arnaud of New York and Paris for allowing us to use the lounging photo of yours truly on the back cover.

My sincere thanks to the reason there is country music, the Grand Ole Opry, along with General Manager Pete Fisher, Marketing Manager Dan Rogers, P.R. ladies Jessie Schmidt & Darlene Bieber; the Ryman Auditorium where I was made happy so often in my life; my dear friend George Gruhn & Gruhn Guitars; Starstruck Entertainment; TNN; and the marvelous Jim Sherraden at Hatch Show Print for all their help and for allowing us the use of these facilities for photos.

From my heart's bottom I appreciate the hard work, enthusiasm, and God-given genius of the following:

Chris Hilicki	Publisher, Creative Director, & Project Producer
Rich Hilicki	President—Dalmatian Press
Susie Garland & Amy Ware (sisters with vision)	Creative Project Managers—Creative Works
Gretchen, Jenny, Robert & Ted	Designers—Creative Works
Gina Rhodes and her team	Creative Director—Dalmatian Press
Andy & Melissa	Art Directors—Dalmatian Press
Kimberly Lanza	Production Director—Dalmatian Press
Mike Rutherford Studio & his great staff	Food, Artist & Nashville Music Scenery Photography
Mike Rutherford	Photographer—Rutherford Studios
Aubrey, Chad, Iwan, & Jim	Assistant Photographers—Rutherford Studios
Jeff Frazier	Artist Photographer—Jeff Frazier Photography
Linda Carman	Food Stylist
Sandra Kingdon	Assistant Food Stylist
Mary Ann Fowkes	Test Kitchen

I gratefully acknowledge the extra effort and assistance of each person at Dalmatian Press, Creative Works, and Rutherford Studios, whose creative input added a greater dimension to this book. As this dream nears reality, let me say that all of you have made this project even more beautiful than I'd imaged it would be. Be proud of yourself! I thank you.

Luv,
Hazel